WOLLATON HALL
AND
THE WILLOUGHBY FAMILY

WOLLATON HALL
AND
THE WILLOUGHBY FAMILY

by

PAMELA MARSHALL

with drawings by

DAVID TAYLOR

Nottingham Civic Society

1999

For Maurice Barley

ISBN 1 902443 05 5

Printed by Technical Print Services Limited, Nottingham, England.

Contents

Illustrations List

Unattributed photographs were taken by the author.

Preface

Following the publication of 'Wollaton Hall, An Archaeological Survey', the Nottingham Civic Society persuaded Pamela Marshall to write and assemble illustrations for a more popular version of the story of the building of the Hall. The new book retains enough material to understand how the building was built, what it was built of and how it functioned; BUT she now adds the human dimension of why was it built, how did it affect the lives of those who lived there and did it make them happy, successful or sad?

The late Professor Maurice Barley, to whom this publication is also dedicated, was one of the first archaeologists to ask these sorts of questions - how did the people live who built the great buildings of our past? - how many bricks did a bricklayer lay each day? - where were the bricks made? - how much did they cost? - how many were used in the construction of the building? - how many hours each week did the bricklayer work and what could be deduced from this sort of information about the society of that time?

Pamela Marshall has explored the lives of the people who lived and worked in the Hall and how the building affected them. By studying their lives, she gives us a new perspective of the building of great houses, their financing and the sheer mental pressure of the scale of such enterprises. It is an absolutely fascinating new dimension to the story of Wollaton Hall and undoubtedly a great deal more remains to be discovered. We should all be grateful to the author for already revealing so much and hope that she will continue her investigation.

Publications are part of the work of the Nottingham Civic Society which promotes new buildings of quality and fine architecture, as well as protecting the very fine heritage of our City. Why not join us, we certainly need your help as commercial pressures continue to build up and progress is often confused with modernism for its own sake, rather than for the benefit of the citizens and the City as a unique place.

Every city needs wonderful and different buildings to make that city different and special. Wollaton Hall is one of those wonderfully different or even eccentric buildings which make Nottingham special.

We hope you enjoy reading the book and trust that it will illuminate and add to the enjoyment of your visit.

ROBERT CULLEN
January 1999

Acknowledgements

Those who have contributed to the completion of this work by their encouragement are too numerous to mention. However, particular thanks are due to Mr. Ken Brand, who read the first draft and whose comments were most useful. He has also seen the book through to publication on behalf of Nottingham Civic Society. Thanks are also due to Mr. Graham Walley and the staff at Wollaton Hall Natural History Museum; to Dr. Dorothy Johnston and the staff of the Department of Manuscripts and Special Collections at the Hallward Library, University of Nottingham; to Dr. Philip Dixon and Dr. Chris Salisbury for taking many of the photographs, and to David Taylor for his excellent drawings. Thanks are also given to the Library of the R.I.B.A., London, to the National Trust and to the Hon. Michael Willoughby, Lord Middleton, for permission to reproduce items in their collections.

PAMELA MARSHALL
January 1999

WOLLATON HALL.

These two Coats of Armes are over the Dore at Wollaton Hall.

Page 223

R. Hall delineavit W. Hollar fecit

Frontispiece

Prologue: A visit to Wollaton Hall

Visitors to Wollaton Hall are often confused. Its elaborate external decoration appealed so much to Victorian taste that the motifs found on it were sometimes copied on Victorian buildings. Wollaton, however, is an Elizabethan house, built between 1580 and 1588. It is essentially a brick house encased in Ancaster stone, which has survived in such excellent condition that it, too, sometimes seems to belie the age of the building. The quarrying of the stone was personally supervised by the architect, Robert Smythson, over four centuries ago and his care seems to have paid off.

Tour of the house: Ground Floor (see illustration 54)

The Georgian Entrance Hall

On entering by the front door, you have to mount a few steps to reach the main floor of the house. Although called the 'ground' floor, it is not really at ground level, for it is raised above a basement which is only semi-subterranean. The windows you see outside on the very bottom floor of the house light this basement, although they are usually high in the walls of the basement rooms, for these were partly dug into the ground. (These are not open to the public).

Once inside, you find yourself in a spacious hallway decorated in Georgian neo-classical style; not what you would expect in an Elizabethan house. In fact the whole entrance area was reworked between 1801 and 1809, opening up a much larger reception space than that which previously existed.

The Great Hall

Carry straight on through double doors, (another Georgian innovation), and enter the Great Hall. Look to your right and you will see a large, carved stone structure supporting a gallery above it. This was the Screen. Before the doorway you have just used was put in, visitors would have entered the Hall from the Screens Passage, the narrow space behind the Screen. In the 16th and 17th centuries, the Great Hall was used for the household at large to take their meals. The Screen divided the Hall from the passage where the food appeared, being brought through three doors still found in the back wall of the passage. Look upwards and notice the carved and painted Hammer Beam Roof. Although original, it was somewhat elaborated during the early 19th century, when the large shields were inserted. In the late 17th century the Great Hall began to take on a different role. It would still be used for gatherings of the whole household, such as morning and evening prayers, but no longer for communal meals. Gradually it came to be regarded as a grand reception area, sometimes used for parties or balls. The double doorways leading straight from the entrance lobby were put in to facilitate this. Another set was put into the opposite wall, linking the Great Hall with another reception room.

The Regency Saloon

Cross the Great Hall and go through these doors and you will find yourself in the Regency Saloon. This room started life as the private Dining Parlour of the Willoughbys. It was a smaller room then, for it was extended towards the west end in around 1832. All the plasterwork and joinery date to this period, and it has been decorated and furnished to show what it would have been like about the middle of the 19th century.

The South State Staircase

Leave by the door in the end wall and you will arrive at the bottom the South State Staircase. Put in during the first decade of the 19th century, this replaced an Elizabethan staircase which was considered old-fashioned. The ceiling was decorated around the turn of the 18th century.

The Georgian Library

Move into the display gallery beyond the staircase. This long room is now full of Natural History exhibits. It started life split into smaller spaces, which were used as bedrooms, and there was a staircase leading out of the house to a courtyard, across which the Tudor stables were probably located. Between 1801 and 1809, these spaces were reworked and combined to make a large Library.

The North State Staircase

Move through this room and turn left and you will emerge at the foot of the North State Staircase. Like its counterpart on the south side of the house, this was also replaced early in the 19th century. Climb the stairs and pause to look at the mural paintings. Like the ceiling of the South State Staircase, they were executed at the beginning of the 18th century. The artists were Sir James Thornhill and Louis Laguerre, a Frenchman. On the wall opposite the window, a doorway was blocked up so as not to disturb the flow of the mural, which depicts the legend of Prometheus. (A similar doorway can still be found on the landing of the South Stairs - see below.)

The Upper Floor

The North Great Chamber

On reaching the top of the stairs, turn right. You will find yourself in the North Great Chamber, the reception room of a formal suite in which Wollaton's builder, Sir Francis Willoughby, envisaged himself receiving Queen Elizabeth. This pipe dream never materialised, although the suite was used by Queen Anne of Denmark, the wife of James I, in 1603. The chamber retains its original shape, but the windows were made narrower during the Georgian period in order to accord with current fashion. (They retain their full width on the outside, so as not to detract from the symmetry of the exterior elevation.) The cast iron fireplace dates to the same period. Under layers of subsequent redecoration, evidence was found for the early 19th-century decoration of the room and this has been restored. At that period, excavations at Pompeii in the Bay of Naples were taking place and it became a fashionable port of call for young men taking a Grand Tour to complete their education. Roman decorative motifs became popular. One of these (albeit a rather unsophisticated one) was to paint false joints, as of stonework, on a plain background, and this might have influenced the rather bizarre decoration of the walls. The background colour is more certainly attributed to Pompeian influence, as 'Pompeii Red' was found extensively in the interior decor of the ancient city and became very popular in the early 19th century.

The South State Bedchamber

The door in the end wall of the Great Chamber will take you into the bedchamber, which was part of the suite. Anne of Denmark slept here in 1603, after which date the room was called 'the Queen's Chamber'. Like all the rooms on the upper floor, it was radically modernized during the first part of the 19th century, and it now houses a Natural History display.

The Screens Gallery, Great Hall and Prospect Room

Come back into the Great Chamber and go through the door immediately on your right. This will bring you on to the Screens Gallery, the upper floor of the Screen, which leads across the Hall to the south side of the upper storey. You get a good view of the Hall and its hammer beam roof from here. Pause and look at the far end of the Hall. High up in the centre of the wall, there is a large clock. This covers a window, exactly like those you can still see at the same level in each of the side walls. These windows overlooked the Hall from the respective landings of the north and south State Stairs, and the one covered by a clock looked out from a very small room off the Elizabethan Long Gallery, which was originally a lavatory. To either side of the clock, you will see a series of very narrow slit-like windows in the wall. These lit spiral staircases, built in the thickness of the wall, which led from the landings of the state stairs and went up to the flat lead roofs of the house, where people walked and admired the views. They also led to the Prospect Room, which sits on top of the Great Hall. The same size as the Hall, it appears to have been used only as a place to walk, look at the view, and perhaps watch hunts taking place in the Park. In the 18th century it was used for dancing, but this had to stop because the floor became unsafe. The Prospect Room is not open to the public for the same reason. As we have seen, the spiral staircase on the left-hand (the north side) was blocked and its doorway removed when the murals were executed on the north State Stair landing, but the one on the right (the south side) still exists.

The organ in the centre of the gallery appears in a drawing of the great Hall published in 1809. It was no doubt used to entertain visitors.

The South Great Chamber

Carry on across the Screens Gallery and the door at the other end will bring you into the South Great Chamber. The room is now obscured by the Natural History displays, but its original purpose was to act as the private sitting or dining room for a very special guest. Had Queen Elizabeth I visited Sir Francis Willoughby, she would have used this room and slept in the bedroom through the door at its west end (to your right: not open to the public). The south state suite was used in 1603 by Prince Henry, the heir to the throne, who accompanied his mother on her visit. They were on their way to London to attend the coronation of James I (the VI of Scotland), who succeeded Elizabeth I.

South Stair Landing and former Long Gallery

Turn left and cross the South Great Chamber and you will emerge on the landing of the south State Stairs. You will see the doorway which leads to the spiral stair to the roof, and also the window overlooking the Hall.

Carry on and you will enter a series of quite small, low rooms. In the original house, you would have entered the Long Gallery, a much taller room, which would have stretched out before you for the whole length of this wing. It was used in the Elizabethan period to take gentle exercise by walking up and down when the weather was inclement. It was heated by two fireplaces and, as we have seen, had a lavatory off it. It would have displayed some of the Willoughbys' proudest possessions, including family portraits. At the beginning of the 19th century the owner of the house, the 6th baron Middleton, was concerned about the small number of rooms, and particularly about the lack of servant's accommodation. He employed the architect Jeffry Wyatville to modernize the house and it was he who was responsible for most of the refurbishments we have seen already. He slit up the Long Gallery into lots of smaller rooms. The reason why the ceilings are so low is that he also placed and extra floor in the upper part of the Gallery, which was divided into rooms for servants to sleep in. He did this in many other parts of the house too. The walls are now blanked out to enhance displays for the Natural History Museum, but if you could see the windows, you would see that only the lower halves are visible, while the upper halves light the new floor above.

Carry on through these rooms and you will emerge at the north State Staircase again. Go down and out of the building.

A walk around the exterior of the house.

As you leave the house, notice the terrace. It was replaced early in the 19th century, and if you look carefully where the handrail meets the wall, you can see the ghost marks of the earlier, Tudor, balustrade. At ground level, turn right. The wide doorway in the turret in front of you, with its heavy door, was a delivery door to the Wine Cellar. There might have been a comparable doorway, now blocked, in the opposite turret on the far side of the stairs, for taking provisions into the kitchens.

Carry on and go through the iron gate on your right into the gardens.

The East Wing

Beneath your feet, the main passage of a Tudor sewer runs toward the garden terrace. There is also a complex of wide passages and a water storage cistern known as the Caves complex. Stand back and face the wall of the house. If you look at illustration 74, it will give you an impression of what lies under the ground.

Now look at the building. In the lower section of the wall you will see smaller windows, which are set high up in the basement. The Wine Cellar is on your extreme right and the other windows lit lodgings for some of Sir Francis Willoughby's servants. You can also see two blocked doorways. The one on the right was never a real doorway: it was made to balance the other on the overall elevation, and you will notice that it is blocked with stone identical with that used on the house. The doorway towards the left was a postern door to the stables: a short staircase led down to it from ground floor level. This was removed between 1801 and 1809 when Wyatville combined most of the rooms in this wing to make the Library. The stone used to block the doorway is White Hollington, not a very good match for the Ancaster Limestone used on the rest of the building. Some of the statues in the grounds, dating from about the same time, had plinths made of Hollington stone and there must have been some left over.

The ground floor rooms in front of you were all originally bedrooms, although the central part of the wing was converted to a Library in the early 19th century. All the windows on the first floor would have belonged to the Long Gallery.

Turn around and, looking away from the house, you will see the lawns, now covered with trees, are D-shaped. This reflects the shape of a bowling green laid out late in the 17th century (see illustration 44). It was surrounded by a ha-ha (a deep ditch) to keep the park deer from entering the garden. The 17th-century painting also shows a banqueting house facing on to the bowling green (illustration 44), but that has disappeared altogether.

The South Side

Move around the corner to the south side of the house, where you will arrive in the formal garden area of the Tudor mansion. There was probably a pond then in the same position as the one today and there would have been parterres (formal beds framed with miniature box hedges). Siberecht's painting shows a rectangular Orangery or glass house towards the eastern end of the formal garden area (illustration 44).

Looking up at the house, this is a good position to view the High Hall and the turret chambers on the leads, which were all used as a recreation area (not open to the public). You can see a stone tablet on the parapet, which records the completion of the house. The room on the first floor was the South Great Chamber destined to act as Queen Elizabeth's private reception room, had she chosen to visit Sir Francis. Her bedroom would have been in the jutting chamber on the left, and this is where Prince Henry slept in June 1603. The room below this one, on the ground floor, was also one of the better bedrooms. It was called the Garden Chamber and later the Duke's Chamber after it was used by the future Charles I (then Duke of York) in 1604. In the centre of the ground floor elevation was the Dining Parlour, later to become the Saloon. The French windows date from the Regency period, as does the terrace: you can see from Siberechts' painting how its predecessor was arranged (illustration 44).

The doorway on the right-hand side of the terrace only dates from the early 19th century. There was always a doorway on the left-hand side, although the one there now is slightly different. The original doorway was a postern door, originally much taller, leading to the garden from the Screens Passage by a short flight of stairs inside the house. When the Saloon was extended c.1832, this was removed and replaced with a flight descending from the terrace into the basement. The door heading was made lower to accommodate a larger window to the Saloon and if you look carefully, you can see where the stonework around the present doorway has been patched up.

The Grounds

Walk past the pond and down the steps to the lower level of the garden. When the house was new, the park would have started where the golf course now begins, but there were orchards here in 1697 (see illustration 44). Moving to the right and turning the corner, you will come across the Camellia House, built c.1823. The cultivation of exotic plants was a fashionable hobby of the rich and the extensive use of iron in Lord Middleton's structure made it a great technical achievement in its day. The gardens in front of it might be where Thomas Willoughby had his 'physick garden' in the late 17th century, and from here you can get a good view of the park and lake, re-landscaped during the 18th century.

The West Wing

Moving along the path and passing through a short tunnel, you will emerge on the western side of the house. The stable block ahead of you was built in 1774. Looking up the hill towards the house, you get a good view of a service wing added to it c.1823 by Wyatville.

Beneath the ground on this side there is another Elizabethan sewer system and a vast underground cellar for the storage of ale, built in the late 17th century. Illustration 72 will help you picture the position of these works. Just beside the steps which lead you back to the front of the building, you can see the only corner of the subterranean Ale Cellar which stands above ground. It has a blocked oval window.

Ill. 1. Wollaton Hall

WOLLATON HALL AND THE WILLOUGHBY FAMILY

Introduction

Ill. 1   No visitor remains unaffected by the sight of Wollaton Hall, rising as it does on the crest of a hill and visible for miles around. With its ornate decoration and central tower, it is unique. Its turreted elevations pierce the horizon and the sun reflects the warm glow of its honey-coloured limestone. Queen Adelaide declared that its beauty was so outstanding that it should be kept under a glass case to protect it from the elements. Others have found its ornamentation, reminiscent of a giant wedding cake, too overpowering. Mark Girouard described it as an unbalanced house built by an unbalanced man with something of the quality of a nightmare. A similar note of censure, rooted no doubt in the enormous cost of the house, crept into Camden's description, published in 1600: 'Sir Francis Willoughby, knight, out of ostentation to show his great riches, built at vast charges a very stately house, both for the splendid appearance and curious workmanship of it'.

Wollaton belongs to the first flowering of the great age of the English country house, which flourished for four centuries before social change finally rang its death knell after the First World War. In an earlier era, builders with sufficient resources would have built a castle or fortified manor and would usually have funnelled considerable funds into the patronage of the Church. But by the end of the 16th century a new epoch was reaching maturity. The Middle Ages were dead and long gone: religious reforms had resulted in a greater emphasis on secular life and a hundred years of general civil order meant that the militarism which had dominated great houses since the Norman Conquest had gone out of fashion. Rich landowners were converting their castles into mansions with pleasure grounds and everyone with the resources to do it wanted to build anew: building great and impressive houses became the passion of the wealthy.

At this time architecture as a profession was still to develop and be recognized. The design of most great houses began as a dream in the mind of a well-endowed patron and was brought to reality by the skill and organization of a master mason working with a team of craftsmen. It was a time of evolution. The builder conferred with acquaintances of his own class, took inspiration from what he had seen on his travels and consulted a growing body of architectural books infiltrating the libraries of European intellectuals. Invariably the patron had strong ideas about what he wanted, but it was the master mason who had experience, practical knowledge and contacts with a pool of skilled craftsmen. These in turn brought ideas and special motifs of their own, developed by themselves or learnt on previous jobs. Each country house was the unique product of such an amalgam, and it was thus that Wollaton Hall came into being.

In 1580 Robert Smythson, 'architector and surveyor', began to oversee work at Wollaton for Sir Francis Willoughby, one of the most complex individuals ever to channel money into architectural ambition. The partnership produced perhaps the most arresting piece of Renaissance architecture in the British Isles. When it was finished in 1588, Wollaton Hall became a wonder of the age: within twenty years it was listed on the agenda of travelling celebrities who wished to see 'what was most remarkable'. But only eight years after the completion of the Hall, Sir Francis was dead. By many, his life might be considered a disaster. He had endured years of bitter wrangling in an unhappy marriage and died without the male heir he longed for. He had fallen seriously into debt, had attempted several business ventures which all failed, had quarrelled rancorously with every member of his family and was rumoured to have been poisoned by his second wife. His one great building, rather than his personal achievements, has ensured the immortality of his name. By contrast, Smythson's name has become synonymous with the blossoming of English Renaissance architecture. He founded an architectural dynasty spanning three generations and his monument records the first application of the term 'architect' to a person, a hitherto unrecognised concept which marks a significant step on the road to acceptance for a developing profession.

Although the exterior of Wollaton Hall remains little altered, changes to the interior have all but eradicated the Elizabethan house. Houses which remain in use over many centuries rarely keep their original form, for each age has its own ideas about how to live. Houses like Hardwick Hall in Derbyshire, with its magnificent Elizabethan interiors, are rare indeed. Hardwick was rather sidelined by the Cavendish family as they concentrated their efforts on their other properties, notably Bolsover and Chatsworth. Perhaps rather unfortunately, the subsequent inhabitants of Wollaton did not neglect to modernise their house, so the present interior is Georgian rather than Tudor. Nevertheless, sufficient architectural clues remain fossilised in its structure to enable a reconstruction of its layout in the late Tudor period. Also, the alterations made over the generations themselves provide a chart of social change, enabling us to see how the lives of Wollaton's inhabitants differed from one century to the next. This was as true for the servants who manned the great house as it was for its owners. The building remained a house until 1924, when Godfrey, 10th Lord Middleton sold it to Nottingham Corporation for £200,000. It was converted to a Natural History Museum which opened on September 1st 1926.

While the Hall remains a curiosity, if we look beyond its flamboyant style into the history of the family which created it, enquiring into the reasoning

Ill. 2. Cassandra Willoughby (1670-1735). Her 'History' of the Willoughby family preserved at second hand many family documents which were later destroyed. Portrait by courtesy of the Hon. Michael Willoughby, Lord Middleton.

behind its design, the way they used the house and the vicissitudes of their everyday lives, Wollaton Hall presents us with a microcosm of life in an Elizabethan and early Jacobean great house. Many surviving contemporary documents allow us to glimpse the nature of life in the mansion's heyday, along with the financial problems bequeathed by Sir Francis to his family as a result of his massive building project. The family history would have remained a rather sterile skeleton, shorn of the flesh which brings historical characters alive, were it not for the contents of private papers, many of them personal letters, which allow us to chart the relationships and fill out the details in the lives of the main protagonists. For much of this detail we are indebted to Cassandra Willoughby, Sir Francis's great great grand-daughter, without whom the contents of these apparently trivial documents would have been lost forever. Many of the original papers were thrown out, almost certainly about 1832 when a new strong-room was created by the 6th baron to store his more valuable documents safely. They had previously lain in the library or the study but were doubtless discarded when the family papers were sorted for transfer to his newly-built muniment room. Many of them would have been in a decayed and fragile condition, but another reason for their destruction must have been their personal nature. Letters recording the arrangements for a wedding, the circumstances of a childbirth or the background to a quarrel were not considered of any interest over two centuries after the event. Fortunately, Cassandra Willoughby was an eminently intelligent woman who was also interested in the history of her forebears. Beginning in about 1690, she had studied 'the Pedigree, old Letters and old Books of Accounts in my brother Sir Thomas Willoughby's study' and by 1709 had written a history of the family. In the pages of her *Account of the Family of the Willoughbys* the contents of many of the documents which were later destroyed are transcribed or related in great detail. Apart from her contribution in rescuing so much of the Willoughby archive, she and her brother also occupy their own place in the history of the house by virtue of important changes they made to it late in the 17th century.

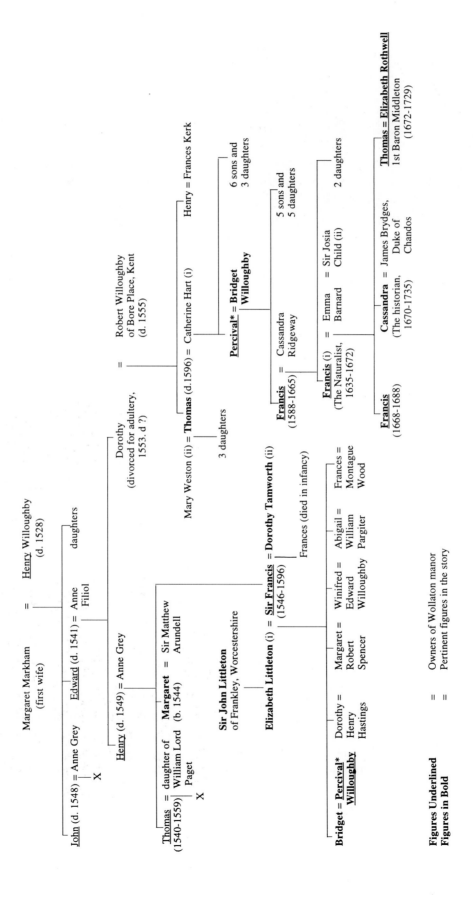

Ill. 3. The Willoughby Family Tree 1528 - 1729

Chapter 1: The Patron

Ill. 4

In 1564 the future looked bright indeed for Francis Willoughby. Aged eighteen, intelligent, educated and enormously wealthy, he was about to marry a girl of his own choosing. However, his character was already showing certain traits, at least partly attributable to his early life, which became more apparent as he grew older and which were later to contribute to domestic strife. So much did Sir Francis' personality impinge on the design of the new hall at Wollaton that it is impossible to understand the building without, in some measure, understanding him. He was well educated in Latin, Greek, Hebrew and arithmetic. To judge from his library list he was a cultured man, perhaps even an intellectual and, significantly, he owned several volumes on architecture. However, he was also wilful, rather arrogant and very jealous of status. He always found personal relationships difficult and was prone to give ear to intrigue, to believe those who had most to gain from misleading him and to suspect those in whom he should have placed more trust. His character was full of contradictions for, while being naturally distrustful of most people, he could be swayed by the unsound advice of a few to the point of gullibility. Much of the unhappiness which clouded his life was manufactured by those around him preying on these weaknesses for their own ends. Above all, he was eager not to be outdone.

Ill. 4. Sir Francis Willoughby (1546-96), the builder of Wollaton Hall. Portrait by courtesy of the Hon. Michael Willoughby, Lord Middleton.

Family Background

Ills. 3 & 5

Francis Willoughby was not *nouveau riche*; he was descended from one of the country's leading gentry families and had a long and honourable pedigree. The rise of the Willoughby dynasty

Ill. 5. The tomb of Sir Henry Willoughby (died 1528) in St. Leonard's Church, Wollaton. Photo by Chris Salisbury

had begun early in the 13th century with Ralph Bugge (a name derived from 'budget', or purse), a merchant from Nottingham who prospered and invested in land. The family adopted a new name on acquiring the manor of Willoughby-on-the-Wolds, also in Nottinghamshire. Between 1314-19 they bought the manor of Wollaton, eleven miles from that estate, from Sir Roger Morteyn and Richard Willoughby married Isabel, Morteyn's heiress. The family increased in status through further marriage alliances and efficient land management, eventually holding lands in Herefordshire, Lincolnshire and Warwickshire, where they obtained a second seat at Middleton around 1435. By the end of the 15th century the head of the family, Sir Henry Willoughby (1451-1528), was a leading figure in Midlands society and was showing an early interest in industry, especially coal mining. He was made a knight banneret by Henry VII for showing his loyalty to the new Tudor dynasty against the pretender Lambert Simnel in 1487. Royal favour extended into the next reign, when he served Henry VIII as Knight of the Body. Although his land holdings extended into several counties, it was in Nottinghamshire that he achieved most prominence in local affairs so that Wollaton remained the principal family residence. Their hall stood near Wollaton church. Despite its survival until 1671, having been converted into estate workers' cottages, there is no detailed record of what it was like. However, a household inventory of 1550 lists 39 rooms as well as outbuildings, showing that it was a very substantial building, no doubt a stout medieval vernacular manor house to which several additions had been made.

Sir Henry's career raised the standing of the family to courtly level but he seemed content with local rather than national prominence. A. Cameron wrote that he raised the family 'to something more than gentry and less than nobility'. There is some evidence to suggest that his heir, Sir John Willoughby, was sympathetic to the Catholic religion. During the religious reforms of Edward VI's reign, when there was wholesale destruction of Roman Catholic artefacts, he was probably responsible for saving an early 14th-century antiphonal, or service book, belonging to Wollaton's church of St. Leonard by hiding it at the hall. Nevertheless, he responded to Henry VIII's request to send help in putting down the Pilgrimage of Grace. Otherwise he kept a low profile politically, steering clear of the intrigues of the age which could prove a minefield for the over-ambitious. Like his forebears, he expanded the Willoughby estates but, perhaps significantly, did not acquire monastic land after the dissolution of the monasteries. At his death Sir John had no direct heir and it was his nephew, another Sir Henry, who inherited the estate. His grandfather had arranged his marriage with Lady Anne, a daughter of the leading Grey family of Bradgate Park, Leicestershire. The Grey alliance was to have its own effect on the builder of Wollaton Hall, for the family was unable to avoid for much longer the effects of turbulent contemporary politics.

Early Life

Francis was the third child of Sir Henry and Lady Anne; his sister Margaret was a couple of years older and his brother Thomas was six years his senior. Francis's mother died when he was a baby and the following year, seven months after inheriting the estate, his father responded, as had all the preceding Willoughbys when necessary, to a royal command to defend the common-wealth. Sir Henry took a contingent of men to Norfolk to help put down Ket's rebellion against the young Edward VI and was killed on Mousehold Heath on 27th August 1549. Eight-year-old Thomas was now a very wealthy young man and was immediately taken into the wardship of his uncle Henry Grey, Marquis of Dorset, later Duke of Suffolk. Margaret and Francis were less valuable catches. After a short stay at Bradgate Park they went to live with their mother's half-brother, George Medley. Though less prominent than Henry Grey, he was a man of substance, with an estate at Tilty in Essex and a London house in the Minories. The children were brought to Tilty on April 21st 1550 with a retinue of twelve servants, bringing thirteen geldings and three carriers with five horses 'with their stuff'. The servants rested for one day before returning without the geldings, but the carriers were sent home the next day. While both guardians took full advantage of their positions by drawing generous expenses from the Willoughby estate, at least they gave the children a good upbringing. George Medley's expenses for the younger children's upkeep show that they were well looked after, even spoiled: the three-year-old Francis had 1d spent on an 'ABC' to teach him his letters, but at the same time 20d was spent on 'a pound of sugar plate and great comfits to make him learn his book'. However, despite the care taken over his education and welfare, the fact that his brother was singled out for special treatment and sent to a more prominent aristocratic household may have had a lasting effect on Francis, who became jealous of status and was always suspicious of being outdone.

In 1554 the Grey connection caused a crisis in the lives of all three Willoughby children. The Duke of Suffolk's abortive plot to thwart the accession of Mary Tudor by elevating his daughter, Lady Jane Grey, to the throne resulted in both their executions. Thomas's wardship was transferred to the Catholic peer, William Lord Paget, but everyone close to the Grey family came automatically under suspicion. Medley was imprisoned in the Tower while his household fell into chaos. It managed to remove to the London house, which had already been raided by Bishop Gardiner's men. The housekeeper, Mrs. Lenton, sent to the bailiff at Middleton for financial help, stating that 'she knew not where to place Master Francis and mistress Margaret Willoughby now that Mr. Medley's house was like to be seized'. No evidence could have been found against Medley, for he was released and things settled down, but these events must have been traumatic for the children.

Queen Mary clearly bore no malice against the Duke of Suffolk's widow, Lady Frances, who was soon back at court, taking with her the young Margaret to finish her education and to effect her 'coming out'. This meant that at the age of seven Francis lost the companionship of his sister, to whom he was very close and who perhaps represented the most stable and secure figure in his life. He was sent away to school in London, Saffron Walden and Cambridge, where he later attended Jesus College. Meanwhile, Margaret was 'so well approved for her good behaviour, etc.' that Lady Frances was confident 'in a short time so to place her about the Queen's Highness, so as to content all her friends, and [which would] also be to her great preferment.' The last prediction was true enough, for she soon found a rich husband, Sir Matthew Arundell. Perhaps about the same time, Thomas Willoughby was married to his guardian's daughter. Paget, having netted the Willoughby fortune, began to angle for the guardianship of Francis as well, accusing Medley of dishonesty and of taking advantage of his young ward, but Medley managed to hang on to Francis's guardianship.

Throughout his childhood Francis had been deprived of a constant companion and sense of real security. He was regularly bundled off to live in strange houses for short periods of time under the protection of a succession of different adults - schoolmasters and housekeepers. He was a younger son; he was to have a good education and be given some start in life, but he was of secondary importance to his brother. In August 1559, against all expectation, this changed. At the age of eighteen young Thomas 'over-heating himself with hunting, he fell sick and died'. Francis suddenly became heir to the Willoughby estates and, consequently, a valuable asset. His wardship was sold to Queen Elizabeth's cousin, Sir Francis Knollys. As Francis approached a suitable age, his guardian naturally proposed to secure his interest in the Willoughby fortune by marrying him off to his own daughter. However, in his short life Francis had suffered a number of traumas: he had lost both his parents, had experienced the execution of one uncle and the imprisonment of another and had suffered the loss of his sister's company shortly after this crucial series of events. It must have seemed as if no one person could be relied on to remain constant and, if nothing else, he had learned distrust. The death of his brother must have made him even more aware of the way in which the management of his family inheritance was regarded as a prize to be fought over by already wealthy but insatiably ambitious men. He was also at just an age to rebel against those authorities who seemed to take more account of him because of his unexpectedly increased status. A combination of these factors led him to dumbfound his family by refusing the match. Knollys sold Francis's wardship back to the executors of his father's will in 1564 and the teenager became a wealthy man in control of his own destiny.

Marriage

Ill. 6. Elizabeth Littleton, Sir Francis Willoughby's first wife. Their marriage was frowned upon by his sister Margaret. Portrait by courtesy of the Hon. Michael Willoughby, Lord Middleton.

The same year Francis made visits to the households of various friends and acquaintances, one of whom was a Mr. John Littleton at Frankley in Warwickshire, the neighbour to his manor of Middleton. Here he was 'sundry times received with great cheer and good entertainment'. In November 1564 he desired his uncle's blessing on his marriage with the daughter of this house, Elizabeth Littleton. He wrote that 'after good deliberation it had pleased God to give him a liking to the young gentlewoman, who had had a good education and was descended from a house of great antiquity, well friended and allied, dwelling near his house of Middleton.' Through the pages of Cassandra's account we can still feel the reverberations caused by this proposal. Margaret was horrified. Spending much of her time at court, she had a clearer idea of who constituted a suitable match for her brother. That he had rejected an alliance with the Knollys family, who were cousins to the queen and influential in the Privy Council, only to marry the girl next door in rural

Warwickshire was incomprehensible. That these negotiations were so far advanced that he and his future father-in-law had already agreed the terms of the marriage contract, before his family were even aware of what was afoot, seemed more sinister. The bride-to-be was around twenty-four years of age, very old to be a spinster still available on the marriage market, suggesting that she commanded an inadequate dowry. Francis was only eighteen. In Margaret's view this was surely a case of an inexperienced youth, not brought up in the expectation of great wealth, being preyed on by a wily family of upstart gold-diggers. In expressing this opinion she did not mince her words. She also held George Willoughby, their uncle, responsible for having procured the marriage 'out of some crafty designs of his own, else he would never have persuaded him [ie. Francis] to proceed so far without consulting any of his friends.' She warned her brother 'not to trust George Willoughby's painted words, nor to let his flattery abuse him so much as to make him think that he was the only person to be of his [ie. Francis's] counsel, for he [Francis] had divers friends that had more care for him, and were better able to advise him.' She concluded sarcastically 'I pray God to send you as good speed, as your haste has been great, which seldom goes together.' The rancour between Francis and Margaret became so great that he accused her of coveting his estate, so that she would oppose his marriage to anybody. She replied that if this had been the case she would never have agreed to the buying out of his wardship, which had required her consent. In her family *History* a century and a half later, Cassandra commented diplomatically that, while Francis had been closer to Margaret than to anyone, 'his sister, being older than he, and by being much together when they were children, she had assumed and gained to herself such a power of governing him that after, when they were grown up, she could not leave off the custom.' Perhaps Francis was in love for the first time; in any case his sister's objections only served to underpin an obstinacy that was to reveal itself throughout his life. Margaret, coming to terms with the inevitable, made some show of making the best of it, expressing a desire to become acquainted with her future sister-in-law and finally wishing them 'happily to match and joyfully to live together'. The marriage went ahead, but the seeds of enmity sowed between the two most important women in Francis's life had firmly taken root.

After this ominous start, matters were made worse by Littleton's failure to pay his full share of Elizabeth's marriage portion. Margaret was not slow to exploit this situation, making frequent enquiries 'to know if Sir John Lyttleton had paid the money, or set the day when he would', and wishing Francis 'better fortune with the rest that is to come than he has hitherto had'. She drove her point ruthlessly home by stating that Littleton's dealing with her brother 'had verified her opinion of him that he was a great dissembler, and for that reason it was that she misliked his matching into that house'. In her *History,* Cassandra was to add her own two-pennyworth, though with typical diplomacy. Referring to a story related in Dugdale's *Antiquities of Warwickshire* concerning the trickery of one Sir John Littleton, she says 'if true, and of the same Sir John Littleton, [this] would give one reason to believe Lady Arundell's thoughts that he were an ill man was but too well grounded.'

Not content with attacking his father-in-law, Margaret lost no opportunity to criticise Francis's wife. Cassandra tells of her copious correspondence with her brother: 'There are many letters ..... which shew that she must have been very much to blame in aggravating Lady Willoughby's faults to Sir Francis, and thereby increasing the uneasiness that was between her and her husband. It appears that she had an inquisitive way of picking up all the little stories that she could of Lady Willoughby and then telling them with advantage to her brother.' Lady Willoughby adopted the only form of defence that seemed open to her, by refusing to have anything to do with her sister-in-law. She wrote to Sir Matthew Arundell entreating him to restrain his wife from carrying out a plan to visit them, pointing out that he could not be 'ignorant what letters his wife had writ ..... in which she would have represented her [ie. Elizabeth] a person fitter for Bridewell than to trouble any honest gentleman's house.' She concluded that she had proof aplenty of the 'ill will she [ie. Margaret] bore herself and children, and she believed her coming now would tend to no other end but to break the good agreement which there now was between her husband and herself.' This 'good agreement' was rapidly becoming wishful thinking. In many respects Lady Willoughby merely played into her opponent's hands by her resolve never to stay under the same roof as Lady Arundell. Margaret played this for all it was worth, frequently reminding her brother of her desire to see him, were it not for Elizabeth's obstinacy, and extending to him her sympathy, expressing 'her trouble that what should be his comfort is his greatest grief'.

If Elizabeth thought that keeping Margaret out of the house would starve her enemy of information which could be maliciously turned against her, she was sadly mistaken. Lady Arundell had certainly recruited the top level of her brother's household staff to act as her informers. Although called servants, these were well-educated men, often distantly related to the family and, since major Tudor households modelled themselves on the royal court, were more like courtiers. Bess of Hardwick had begun her career in this way. They acted as secretaries and managers, while lower levels of the serving classes actually did the physical work. Cassandra informs us that at Wollaton a group of the higher servants kept up a concerted attack on their mistress, which Margaret might have been orchestrating from a distance:

> 'There is in this year, A.D. 1572, a long and very particular account in writing of a scene of great villainy laid by Ithel, Catesby, Marmyon, Pardia, Barthol and Widdison, all servants of Sir F[rancis] Willughby, who had plotted together to defame their lady, and thereby make a breach between her and Sir Francis. Among these wicked servants Ithel seems by this account to have been the

worst. 'Tis there noted down that he took great pains to have drawn Squire, another of Sir F[rancis] Willloughby's servants, to have been in their cabal, but they could not prevail with him, who would always assert his Lady's innocency and pity her misfortunes.'

In June 1572 Elizabeth's father complained by letter to Sir Francis that Catesby and Marmion 'spread slanderous reports of his daughter'.

Squire opted to join Lady Willoughby's camp and left an account describing his mistress's 'unquiet life through Ithel and his companions dealing against her and belying her to her husband'. Lady Willoughby confided to him that Sir Anthony Strelley, a neighbour of the Willoughbys, was overheard to remark 'I am heartily sorry for that poor gentlewoman's miserable case, there being certain varlets who villainously seek her utter undoing'. Squire also gave an account of Lady Arundell's tactics in quizzing her informers. Having been sent to London on business, Squire waited on Lady Arundell to see if she wanted any messages bringing back to Nottingham. 'After a little astronomical talk, and about mathematical books in the Italian tongue, etc., she made large enquiry after her sister, the Lady Willoughby, viz., what company she kept etc.' Lady Arundell's preamble shows the level of education attained by these servants. They were accustomed to moving in exalted circles and the same Squire made it his business to seek an interview with the Countess of Warwick in which he advised her to discount any stories she might have heard from Lady Arundell defaming his mistress. This provoked a broadside from Margaret to Sir Francis, excusing Ithel and asserting that Squire was 'a dissembling knave'.

Margaret did not have it all her own way, however, for Sir Francis often wrote to defend his wife during the early part of their marriage. In one letter to his sister he stated that 'upon examination [he had] found Ithel guilty of telling stories and making lies of his wife' and in another he puts a defamation at the door of 'Catesbie's wife, who is scant honest'. However, he did not dismiss his servants and, like water dripping at a stone, their interference eventually had the desired effect. Had Sir Francis been more discerning in the selection of the top rank of his household staff he might have saved his family considerable unhappiness. One of the troublemakers, Marmion, had previously been employed by Sir Francis but had left to serve the Countess of Shrewsbury, the famous Bess of Hardwick. Marmion's letter of application to return to Wollaton survives. It is rambling, long-winded and obsequious but, more significantly, shows that he was considered at the time to be at the very centre of the disquiet which was rocking the Shrewsbury marriage to its foundations:

'I told your worship at your last being at Haddon of a broyle or kynd of tragedy betwixt my Lord and Lady of late, wherin, as alwayes in maner hertofore, my Lorde hathe made me playe a parte, so I thinke the tragedy would not hould if I be lefte out'.

Sir Francis would have been wise to steer clear of Marmion, but he was always prone to flattery. Marmion presented himself as the victim of Lord Shrewsbury's malice because of his position as the confidant and very prop of Lady Shrewsbury, Sir Francis's exalted friend and kinswoman. He also allowed himself a certain amount of name-dropping, implying that he could easily get a position with the Lord Treasurer or the Earl of Leicester, but would prefer a quieter life. Marmion and his fellows seem to have enjoyed more success in gaining Sir Francis's ear than his own wife.

To make matters worse, Lady Willoughby was not in good health. In sixteen years she had twelve children and, although the couple brought six daughters to healthy maturity, they had less luck with boys. The fact that Elizabeth was usually either pregnant or recovering from childbirth, combined with the additional stresses of her unenviable situation, made her frequently ill. In 1574 she wrote of her desire that her physicians might 'give her something, either to help or else dispatch her quickly, for she thinks death would be a thousand times more welcome than to live as she now does, continually sick'. The Wollaton household accounts record regular payments to Dr. Richard Smith, who also acted as physician to the queen, and his attendances on Lady Willoughby often included recompense for his travel to and from London. The midwife and the apothocary, Mr. Bannister, were also kept in brisk business. In 1574 the latter was paid 20s 4d (about three weeks' wages for a skilled craftsman) in a single transaction. The order included diacodium, an opiate made from poppy-heads taken in syrup form. In the same year Mrs. Bannister supplied 'swooning water for my mistress' at a charge of five shillings, as well as other remedies.

While the apothecary's bills would cover the needs of the whole household, there is some evidence that Sir Francis began to baulk at the cost of his wife's ailments. In a letter of May 1575 to Dr. Smith, related by Cassandra, one can detect a note of scepticism, particularly concerning the doctor's advice that Lady Willoughby should take the waters at Buxton. Sir Francis countered that Lady Willoughby's intemperate nature was largely responsible for her condition:

> And whereas he [ie. Dr. Smith] advised her to live in a wholesome air and eschue disorder in her diet and perturbations in her mind, for the air he writes [ie. Sir Francis] that he thinks she will not mislike the place where he is disposed to dwell, being unwilling himself to be in any air which they could find hurt by, but in this point he desires she will consider her duty rather than to suffer herself to be guided by self will. For her disorder in diet and the perturbations of her mind, she only must help that; for his part he would not give her any just occasion of trouble if reason might take place, and wilfull will be laid aside.

The last is a reference to Lady Willoughby's outbursts of temper. The Willoughby documents go some way to representing her as a sort of neurotic, yet it is clear that her determination to have some say in her own destiny was often frustrated. As a result there were occasionally scenes. Lady Willoughby comes through as a woman who at least held her own, but this was also turned against her, being considered unfeminine. Margaret, as usual, was liberal with her advice to her brother:

> the next time she falls into those rages that he should send for her father to come to her, and they [i.e. father and daughter] should both go with him home and board there with a convenient number of servants, until such time as she should have lost her wilfullness, and would apply herself to please him [i.e. Sir Francis].

Cassandra summed up the Willoughbys' relationship with her usual understatement: 'By these and many more copies of letters that are in the library it appears that Sir Francis and his Lady lived very unhappily together'.

The Household at the Old Hall

Against the background of his private life, Sir Francis had a role to play in provincial society. Apart from the manor houses at Wollaton and Middleton, he maintained houses in Nottingham, Coventry, Kingsbury (Warwickshire) and London. He kept around fifty servants and spent somewhere in the region of £1,200 per annum on household expenses in an age when a skilled craftsman might expect to earn £17 a year. In November 1572 a bill paid to a London grocer amounted to £22 8s 10d, with an extra 6d paid out in tolls for the three horses which carried the goods to Nottingham. The order contained luxury spices including pepper, nutmegs, ginger, cinnamon, mace, cloves, dates, prunes, raisins, currants, liquorice, aniseed, almonds, and rice as well as 190 pounds of sugar of varying quality. The Wollaton cook was apparently stocking up for Christmas. Fish and wine were brought in from Hull, but much of the produce which ended up on Sir Francis's table would have come from his own lands. At this time of his life money does not appear to have been a problem and he easily adopted the life-style of the nobility. There are records of generous payments of alms, for sumptuous clothing, musical instruments and for entertainment. Sir Francis spent at least £20 a year on musicians' wages and occasionally had companies of visiting players under noble patronage perform at Wollaton Old Hall.

Some orders laid down for his Coventry house show how strictly Sir Francis liked his household to be run. Prayers were said before dinner and supper and 'the children do go to bed straight after eight o'clock at night and are made ready before eight o'clock in the morning'. Also 'that the servants be not gadding into the town, but give their attendance at dinner and supper, and all other times'. We have already seen that Sir Francis kept an elite class of servants; a household order of about 1572 for the old hall at Wollaton gives us some insight into the duties of the next class down. It records the rules of the house for the benefit of the staff, giving a fascinating insight into domestic routine at that time. It was styled on similar orders which were current in noble households and first deals with the duties of the usher, one of the most important officers. He was to supervise the cleaning of the Hall and to make sure no dogs were allowed in. He was also to monitor all visitors so that they could be dealt with according to their rank:

> that if they be of the better sort, notice may be given to the master, or some head officer that they may be entertained accordingly. If of the meaner sort, then to know the cause of their coming ..... to the end that they may be dispatched and answered of their business, provided always that no stranger be suffered to pass without offering him to drink, and that no rascall or unseemly person be suffer'd to tarry there.

A large portion of the usher's duties was concerned with overseeing meals in the Great Hall. Two main meals were served; dinner at about 11.00am and supper at about 5.00pm and these took place in two separate rooms. The master and his guests would eat in the Dining Parlour, while the remainder of the household, including the servants of visitors, would eat in the Hall. The usher had to see all went smoothly, that torches and fires were laid on in the Hall in winter, and that each sitter was placed according to his or her rank. The usher carried a badge of authority, 'a little fine rod in his hand ..... whereby he is to be known of all strangers to be the usher'. The lower status servants such as stable grooms, pages and boys, waited at table on the other servants, then ate up the left-overs themselves, although the usher had authority to summon more food from the kitchen for them if necessary. If numbers to be catered for were unusually high, perhaps owing to an influx of visitors, the usher could bring in extra staff:

> If any great press of strangers shall be, then three or four of the meanest sort of servants, as namely the slaughterman, the carter, and some of the best grooms of the stable or such like, are to be appointed by the usher to attend in t'hall.

The smooth running of the meal was entirely down to the usher; he saw that the attendants brought 'anything that shall be wanting', whilst never compromising his own position of authority by bringing anything himself. He also had to moderate rowdiness:

> if there be any stubborn persons, he is to expell them out of the hall, and to

command all men at dinner and supper time (if any great noise shall be) to keep silence, saying with a loud voice, "Speak softly, my masters."

After the meal was finished and the grooms, pages and boys had had their share, the usher was responsible for overseeing the gathering up of left-overs. These were kept under lock and key in an alms table, a sort of sideboard, 'to be distributed among the poor such days as shall be appointed.' Lastly, he was to see that there was no smuggling of food. The quality of fare served up in the Dining Parlour (sometimes called the Chamber or Great Chamber) would have been rather superior to that served in the Hall, so the usher was

> diligently to see that no meat filched forth of the chamber be brought into the hall ...... nor is he to suffer any filchen through the hall from the buttery, kitchen, or such like places. For he is an officer of great trust and credit, and next to the usher of the great chamber (if any be) in degree above either cooke, butler, yeomen of the chambers, or porter.

The butler, with the assistance of the under-butler, was responsible for laying the tables, cleaning, lighting and heating the Dining Parlour, overseeing the washing up and, above all, organising the provision and serving of drink in good condition. He was to 'have good regard to the cleanness of his linen, and likewise to provide for cards and dice, wherof he is to have the profit.' The under-butler, like the usher, had some responsibility for discipline within the household. He was to make sure that all staff ate in the Hall, so that no one got extra food by hanging around the kitchen, but he had some discretion in allowing rations of bread and beer to go to certain other destinations, such as the nursery, bakehouse or kitchen. Above all, he was to police the distribution of ale:

> to suffer no household servant to remain tippling, or to be at all in the buttery [where the ale was kept]; but whosoever is disposed to drink to be served at the hatch, and so to depart.

The opportunities for the household to be served with beer at the hatch, it has to be said, were not ungenerous. It was open from 8-9am, 10-11am, all through dinner, then again in the afternoon between 2-3pm. It was then shut till supper was served at 5pm and remained open till 9pm, after which hour it was

> by no means to be opened that night without speciall cause. The discretion of that officer is to forsee that no filching of bread or beer be suffer'd, nor yet any want where reason doth require ...... for it is an office of good credit and great trust.

The Country Gentleman

In 1566, only two years after his marriage and when he was still only twenty, Francis must have suffered some disappointment when he learnt from his father-in-law, John Littleton, how narrowly he had missed being knighted. The queen had been staying at Kenilworth and had drawn up a list of local worthies singled out for the honour, including Francis and Sir John himself. Francis had just left the county. On August 24th Littleton wrote that 'if he had not so suddenly departed ... he would have made his daughter a lady, for he was sought for but could not be found within an hour after he was gone, when there were six knights made.' As someone who was always conscious of status, this must have been particularly irksome.

Almost ten years later the management of his estates was still prosperous, despite some fall in the revenues from the coal pits. With his income assured, his household running to strict order (for he was 'very regular in his family') and his daughters still too young for him to be embroiled in negotiations for their marriage, Francis Willoughby would have had a great deal of time to pursue the life of a country gentleman. There is little evidence that he enjoyed outdoor pursuits, although his wife, in a brief interlude of peace, chose for him and sent him a hat 'which is of the newest fashion, and ..... a very good fashion for him, because it is not high crowned, so that when he rides a hunting he may never pull it off.' He had a very good library and he might have preferred intellectual diversions. Cassandra speaks of 'a great many pious discourses writ by him, and several sermons which he made for his own chaplains to preach', although she did not choose to transcribe them. His great, great grand-daughter concluded, with more than a little bias, that he 'appears to have been of a very mild, sweet disposition, and a lover of hospitality, but a little too apt to be imposed on by stories from his servants.' Despite his ample income and a host of top level attendants, we are told that Willoughby himself 'was very exact in keeping the account of his income and his expenses'. We can detect a hint of meanness in his attitude towards his wife's expenditure, especially as their relationship deteriorated. In March 1575 Elizabeth was staying in their London house with the children when he sent horses to convey them to Middleton. Elizabeth must have refused to go, for Willoughby wrote to a servant expressing his disappointment, although his wish to see his children seemed small in comparison with his concern about how much his wife was spending: 'He knows not the meaning of this, unless it be to increase his charges, and if that should exceed the rate he was contented to allow, it would be hardly gotten at his hands'.

Around the age of thirty, Willoughby perhaps began to feel that life was passing him by a little. Entertaining and being entertained by others would have been an important part of his social life and he was friendly with the neighbouring Earls of Rutland and Huntingdon as well as the local gentry. However, in view of his sister's prominent position at court, he might have moved in wider aristocratic circles were it not for his wife's refusal to share her sister-in-law's company. It is perhaps significant that from about this time onwards his marital problems began to escalate.

In June 1575, another opportunity for social recognition seemed to open up. Ill. 7 Elizabeth I was to be feted most extravagantly at Kenilworth by her favourite, the Earl of Leicester. By now the queen's skills in public relations had resulted in a cult of public adoration in which she was hailed as *Gloriana*. Perhaps Willoughby fostered courtly ambition; he certainly seems to have felt ready for some new challenge. He removed to Middleton to be near the celebrations and, anxious to make an impression on the queen, received the following advice from his uncle, the same George Willoughby who had introduced him to his wife:

> (the) servants need only to have plain livery coats, but ..... the number of servants should in no wise be less than fifty, as well because heretofore he had not shewed himself to the Queen, as also that his estate was very well known both to her majesty and to the whole counsel to be nothing inferior to the best. For himself ..... he cannot make less than three suits of apparel, for he is well assured that his attendance will be expected a week.

Although it is not recorded, his knighthood was almost certainly conferred on this occasion. He also seems to have invited the queen and her retinue to stay at his house, probably at Middleton, and he was led to expect a visit. Sir Francis Knollys, his old guardian whose daughter he had slighted, wrote somewhat curtly, warning him to look to the provisioning of his house:

> Her majesty is determined to tarry two days at your house, that is to say tomorrow night and Thursday all day, whereof I thought it good to advertise you betimes. Wherefore I think it best for you not to defray Her Majesty, but rather that you should give her some good present of beefs and muttons, and to keep a good table yourself in some place, if you have any conven-ient room for it, two messe of meat. But do herein as you shall think best, but you had need to consider how your provision of drink etc. may hold out.

Ill. 7. Elizabeth I

The queen had received three invitations at Kenilworth. She went to the other two houses, at Lichfield and Worcester, but not, in the event, to Middleton. As the whole project was clearly a last minute arrangement, it may be that she simply changed her mind. However, Middleton, like Wollaton, was an old-fashioned medieval manor house. Neither would have suited the requirements of Elizabeth's court on progress, and this could have been a factor in the cancellation. This must have dwelt on Sir Francis's mind and it is likely that the germ of the decision to rebuild his principal seat dates from this time.

Separation

If Sir Francis was feeling side-tracked in the first league of fashionable society, he had the dubious consolation of knowing that he was not entirely forgotten by it. Thanks to his sister, the latest gossip concerning himself and his wife's behaviour was regularly aired. During the remainder of 1575 and the two following years the gossips must have been well furnished, for matters between the couple went from bad to worse. After eleven years of unhappiness it seems that Elizabeth had given up any outward pretence of 'good agreement' between herself and her husband. A correspondence between Sir Francis and his father-in-law, containing complaints about her on the one hand and excuses and mollifying words on the other, cover the entire length of the marriage, but at this time they begin to take on a new accent. Sir Francis deplores the fact that Elizabeth's 'forward humour', previously kept a 'secret sorrow ..... was become so public'. In a row which took place before their guests, including Sir Fulke Greville, in the Long Gallery at Kingsbury, she told Sir Francis 'I will blaze your arms and make you better known'. She also harangued him in front of the servants. Sir Francis kept a female fool, Mary, before whom Lady Willoughby declared that it was she (Elizabeth) who was kept 'as a fool, to jest and flout at'. Cassandra describes Lady Willoughby as 'a woman of wit and virtue, but of a turbulent spirit and ungovernable passions ..... which made her say very provoking and vexatious things to Sir Francis'.

Elizabeth's behaviour was extreme but must have resulted at least in part from the frustration she suffered, desperately unhappy, yet universally blamed for the poor relationship because it was considered the woman's place to submit entirely to her husband. Although she gives no details, Cassandra reports that Sir Francis wished to alter the terms of their marriage settlement, which Lady Willoughby resisted. The same George Willoughby who had introduced Sir Francis to Elizabeth now advised him to 'banish his wife from him if ..... she would not at last yield to pass the fines'. A number of increasingly public events contributed to the couple's eventual break-up. Sir Francis began to suspect that his wife's friendship with Lady Stanhope had more to do with her liking for Sir Thomas Stanhope and there was some scandal and argument over her possessing the latter's miniature portrait. About the same time, the quiet village of Wollaton must have witnessed unwonted consternation when Margaret finally came to stay. Elizabeth flounced off to the vicarage and, after much to-ing and fro-ing of messages, returned to the hall but, 'upon her coming into the house she called his sister abominable names and swore she would neither eat, drink or sleep till she was revenged of her'. In another incident Sir Francis left Elizabeth in the house at Kingsbury while he returned to Nottingham. As soon as he left she attempted to dismiss some of the male servants whom she regarded as the enemy, but they refused to go. On confronting them in person she found one of them, Cludde, carrying a sword and sent others to raise the entire town, claiming she was about to be murdered. She finally insisted on an armed escort to the vicarage, where she sought protection.

Elizabeth had threatened to leave on many occasions, claiming she had 'friends who would not see her destitute'. She seems to have gone home to her father several times, although her appearance was not always welcomed. In a letter of November 1578 Sir John complains to Sir Francis of his daughter having turned up without warning, stating roundly 'he thinks fit to let her understand that he [ie. Sir John] is not well, and the sight of her will not mend, but greatly disquiet him, and therefore he trusts never to see her more.' The crunch very probably came in February 1579 when, leaving her in their Coventry house to see to business in London, Sir Francis set down a strict set of rules for governing the household in his absence, making sure there would be no repetition of the Kingsbury incident. The servants Cludde and Draycot were to have complete authority while Lady Willoughby should 'have no authority to command anything in the house except necessary diet for herself'. The order rendered her a virtual prisoner: 'she shall have nothing to do with the children, but that they shall be ordered by such as I shall appoint for that purpose', and she was to be in bed by 9.00pm, when 'nobody must be in the great chamber, but that the fire be raked up and the door locked'. Before he left, Lady Willoughby remonstrated with Sir Francis vigorously, stating that 'who ever would take upon them to order her children in her presence, she would mischief'. She pleaded to stay at an inn until some friends could come and take her away and, finally, 'upon his denying her that, she fell into a most violent passion, threatening to make away with herself, and being denied a knife would have struck her scissors into her belly if she had not been prevented'. She later left the house and was locked out, writing to her husband from a house provided for her by the mayor and aldermen of Coventry, 'in want of all necessaries, having no apparel but what was upon her back, nor any money to bear her charges', and seeking a reconciliation.

We do not know what passed during the following months, but there were probably constant negotiations. The position of a separated married woman was unenviable at that period. Even the formidable Bess of Hardwick, who had relatively independent means from previous widowhoods, found the going tough when she separated from the Earl of Shrewsbury. It is not surprising that Elizabeth began to rue her situation, but Lady Arundell was keen that Sir Francis should not weaken. She warned her brother that:

> her gossips give out that she [ie. Elizabeth] will use all the means she can to come to his presence and use speeches of great submission, although she means not to perform them. And that the mayor and citizens of Coventry have promised her so diligently to solicit the matter, that there is no heart so hard as not to be moved to pity, much less his, whose natural disposition is to be courteous.

In November 1579 Sir John suggested that he and Sir Francis should meet man to man to sort out the differences and effect a reconciliation, apparently to no avail. A month later they were thrashing out the terms of separate maintenance. Her father asserted:

> she can't have less than a gentlewoman to attend her, a nurse for her young son, a maid to help the nurse and to be laundress to them all, a boy needful about the nurse and to make his lady's fires, and a serving man to wait upon his Lady. And for their tabling he trusts Sir Francis will allow for his wife sixteen pence a day, and for each of the servants eight pence a day, and for wages he thinks he can't give less than fifty-three shillings and four pence a year a-piece to the woman nurse and the man, and to the laundress and boy twenty-six shillings and eight pence a-piece. He leaves it to Sir Francis to name what he will for apparel for his wife and little son ..... and what money he will allow her for other needful expenses. He thinks it will also be needful for her to have a couple of geldings to use when she shall have occasion to ride.

The Germ of an Idea

It is very likely that by the time these sorry events were accelerating towards their irreversible conclusion Sir Francis was already setting in motion the groundwork for a scheme designed to restore his standing in the eyes of the world. While at once longing to turn his back on the rude buffetings of a society where he was prey to petty gossip and was rapidly becoming a laughing stock, this *milieu* paradoxically represented the very people whose respect he most desired. Turning to architecture to restore his bruised ego was a perfect solution. Having had enough of publicity, this pursuit could be carried on in isolation, allowing him to remain aloof. It must have appealed to his preferred interests, for it involved those skills he prided in himself; intellect and taste. Best of all, the end product would make his statement for him. It would defy the gossips and restore to him the respect and status he deserved. This was to be no run-of-the mill gentleman's residence. This must be a house that would make people sit up and take notice. It must convey dignity, status, even learning.

It must stun. He no longer had a lady to stand at his side, but he could provide a place fit to receive another lady, one who need only pass a single night under his roof to stop the tongues and correct the injustices he suffered. In short, he resolved to build a house fit for a queen.

In the meantime, however, if the terms suggested by Sir John Littleton for the maintenance of his daughter were ever agreed upon, they were not kept. Two years later Elizabeth reported that she 'had suffered great travail of body and trouble of mind, wandering from place to place and depending wholly for relief upon the borrowing of friends'. Sir Francis's building project was still in its first stages when he was plunged into deep depression by the news that his wife had decided to petition the queen, informing his father-in-law that 'he laments his misfortunes, and wishes for death, rather than to continue so vexatious a life'. He was perhaps vexed further when, in 1582, Queen Elizabeth decreed that Lady Willoughby should receive £200 a year from him.

Chapter 2: The Building Process

The Architect-Surveyor

Ill. 8

Robert Smythson was probably the son of a master mason from Westmorland but little is known of his early life. During the 1560s he worked on a building project, probably at Caversham near Reading, for Sir Francis Knollys, Francis Willoughby's guardian. In March 1568 he arrived at Longleat in Wiltshire to work on Sir John Thynne's famous great house. By this date Smythson was well established in his craft. He brought with him his own team of five workmen and carried references from Humphrey Lovell, Master Mason to the Queen, recommending that he should have sixteen pence per day and 'a nag kept at your worship's charges', the equivalent of the modern company car. He is unlikely to have been involved in the overall design of Longleat, but was one of two principal masons employed there. His colleague, Allen Maynard, was a Frenchman, a talented stone-carver who must have brought designs inspired by his considerable continental experience. Smythson doubtless learned a great deal from Maynard and throughout his life he made a collection of drawings, plans, elevations and decorative devices of all sorts, picked up during the course of his work and travels. Smythson and Maynard were responsible for a large part of the carved detail on the facade at Longleat where Smythson worked, with some interruptions, until 1580. Between about 1576 and 1578 he also remodelled the fourteenth-century castle at Old Wardour in Wiltshire. This was a conversion of the type becoming common amongst the late Tudor aristocracy, as castles were increasingly turned into more fashionable country houses. The building belonged to Sir Matthew and Lady Arundell and it was no doubt they who introduced him to Sir Francis Willoughby, about the very time Sir Francis's own architectural ambitions were taking shape.

An inscription on Wollaton Hall records that construction started there in 1580. Since the first two years of the building accounts are missing, there is no absolute proof that Smythson was involved from the start, although the circumstantial evidence is overwhelming. He left Longleat in 1580 and by 1582 he was general overseer of the works at Wollaton, his status reflected in the fact that he was always referred to as 'Mr.' There

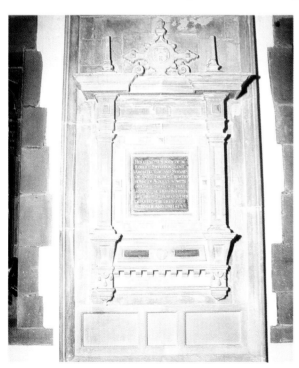

Ill. 8. Robert Smythson's monument, Wollaton Church. Photo by Chris Salisbury.

is no record of his being elsewhere during the intervening period. He certainly saw construction work at Wollaton through to its completion and then stayed on with the Willoughby family as a sort of general manager and administrator until his death in 1614: some of the household inventories, for example, are in his hand. He and his wife must have settled well in Wollaton and decided that they had had enough of moving, but that is not to say he had given up the building trade. On the contrary, his career had reached such a level that he could afford to settle and act as a well-respected consultant to the gentry and nobility in the East Midlands region. He went on to design the New Hall at Hardwick for the Countess of Shrewsbury, the famous Bess of Hardwick, as well as Worksop Manor for her family and there are several other important houses in the area whose designs are attributable to him.

In 1585 he had set his son John to work as a labourer at Wollaton for a few months to gain basic experience before beginning his training as a mason. In 1612 the mature John was following closely in his father's footsteps, being appointed to supply the design and oversee the rebuilding of Bolsover Castle, Derbyshire, for the Cavendish Family. Despite advancing years, Robert might have had a hand in this design. Just as Robert had stayed with the Willoughbys, so John also remained with his Cavendish patrons as a manager with the title bailiff. However, by the third generation a subtle change becomes apparent. John's son Huntingdon succeeded his father as bailiff to the Cavendishes and took over supervision of the Bolsover works in 1629, but never trained as a mason. He also married into the gentry, an indication of the way in which the Smythsons had risen socially above their craft roots within three generations.

Robert Smythson's memorial in Wollaton church recorded his profession as 'Architector and Survayor unto the most worthy house of Wollaton with diverse others of great account'. At this time, however, the word architect was not used in its modern sense: the association of a single individual with the conception and design of a great building would have to wait until the next century. In the context of the 16th century most patrons considered themselves to be prime movers in the pattern of their brainchild. The craftsmen they employed were expected to carry out the grand plan and supply the detail, but were hardly credited with the outcome. How far, then, was Robert Smythson in control of the design and how far was he merely carrying out the orders of Sir Francis? We can compare Wollaton with Smythson's later work, study the documentation and, always bearing in mind what we can glean about the personalities of the men involved, might make informed guesses as to who was suggesting what.

The Design Takes Shape

We are fortunate in that Smythson drew a plan (called a platt in 16th-century terminology) of the ground floor of the hall which a recent survey has shown   Ill. 9

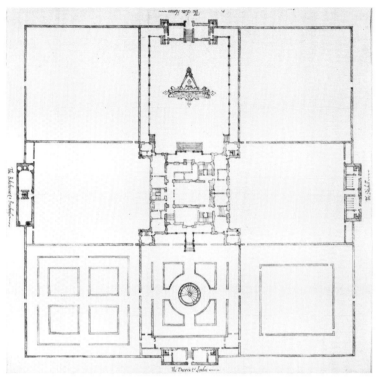

Ill. 9. Smythson's platt, or design drawing of the house and its immediate grounds. British Architectural Library, R.I.B.A., London [Smythson I/25(1)]

to be accurate in almost every detail, but not quite all. This tends to confirm that it was drawn in advance of building and had to be altered in one small respect as unforeseen conditions arose on site. The plan would have been drawn up after considerable consultation with Sir Francis. Rather than being seen as a working drawing, its purpose was more likely to give the patron an idea of what his house would be like. The practice of making a small wooden model of the proposed design was just beginning and it is possible this might also have been done, but since the early records have been lost and no model survives, we can only speculate about this.

Smythson's plan shows that the house and its immediate grounds and outbuildings were all considered to be part of a supremely symmetrical design. The house itself stands in the very centre of a grid formed by nine squares, the eight surrounding squares containing grounds or ancillary buildings to complement it. The square immediately to the north, the front of the house, was to consist of a courtyard entered by a gatehouse and flanked by an arcaded covered walkway on either side. This would provide an impressive approach for the visitor. On the south side, three squares in a row were to be given over to formally laid-out gardens with direct access from the house, via a terrace, from an informal or postern doorway. A long thin rectangular outbuilding was planned along each side of the site and the labels attached to these buildings give a clue as to the use of two of the remaining four squares. To the north we have already noted the gatehouse while to the south of the formal gardens a dairyhouse was to be built. The stables were to be on the east side, so the eastern square probably represented a courtyard, with quick access to and from the house by another postern door. Within the house the services were located on the west side and we find, logically, that the outbuilding on this side was to be a brewhouse cum bakehouse, so we may presume the square in the centre of the west side formed a service courtyard. The bread and ale would be brought across the yard and into the house by two doorways, one to the service area and another directly into the Ale Cellar. The remaining two squares on either side of the entry courtyard on the north side serve no purpose other than to complete the symmetry of the overall plan and it was possibly intended that these should be landscaped to enhance the approach to the house.

Looking more closely at the plan of the house itself, we find that, externally at least, this too was completely symmetrical. It consists of a square with an additional square tower attached to each corner. However, looking even more closely, we can see that the central block is only square because it includes terraces on the north and south sides. The north and south facades are offset to accommodate the terraces, so at each corner a chamber juts out, then the   Ill. 1, 10 & 17

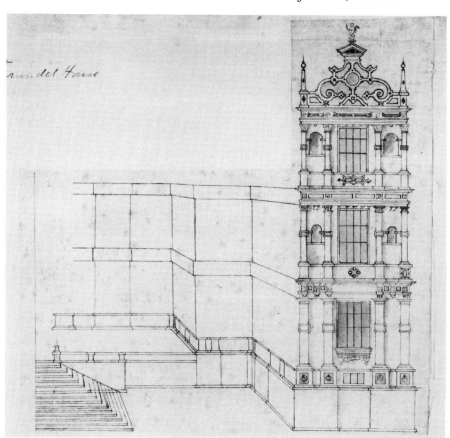

Ill. 10. *A perspective drawing by Smythson, thought to be the earliest English example of its kind, showing a corner of Wollaton Hall. British Architectural Library, R.I.B.A., London [Smythson I/25(2)]*

adjoining tower juts out further. The result is that, instead of a flat front, these facades look more articulated, catching light and shade, and are made more interesting. The use of large bay windows produced a similar effect at Longleat, but at Wollaton the technique was taken further and was used again at Hardwick. A drawing by Smythson of one of the corners at Wollaton is thought to be the earliest architectural elevation drawn in perspective by an English architect.

Ill. 11   Many Elizabethan houses were rather long and thin in plan: sometimes they were modelled on the shape of a letter 'E' and sometimes they consisted of wings surrounding a central courtyard. The compression of the plan at Wollaton into a compact, symmetrical shape, particularly with the addition of a tower at each corner, reflects the influence of a French writer, Jacques Androuet du Cerceau, whose name appears on Sir Francis's library list. His books, *Petits Habitations* (1560) and *Les Plus Excellents Bastiments de France* (1576) had become very popular. Among the Willoughby papers there is an undated plan which was clearly copied from one included in du Cerceau's *Petits Habitations*. It is not clear who drew it, but it probably dates to between 1577 and 1580 and must represent a period when Sir Francis was casting about for ideas. It

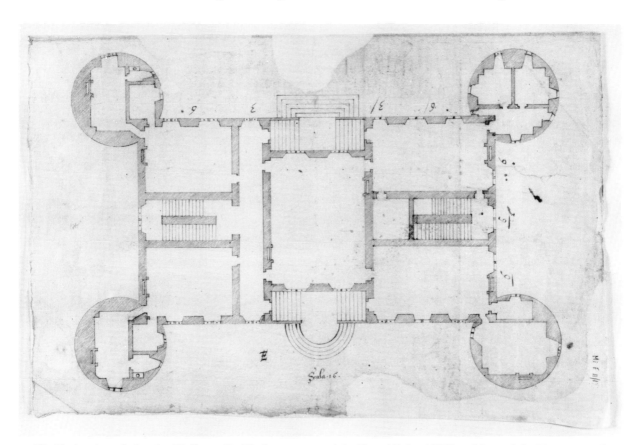

Ill. 11. *A rejected plan for Wollaton Hall? By courtesy of the Hon. Michael Willoughby and the University of Nottingham Library.*

shows a great hall in the very centre, a pair of opposing state staircases and corner towers with sub-divided rooms in them. The final plan, dealt with in more detail in chapter 3, was much more complex but not essentially dissimilar.

The Organization of the Workforce

The undertaking of a great building project was rather different in the 16th century from today. Nowadays the work is usually put out for tender, a contract is drawn up with the firm of builders selected and the whole operation monitored by the architect who designed the plan. A similar method, called 'great', was not unknown then; occasionally a master mason would undertake to build a house under contract but this method was very rarely adopted and usually only applied to much more modest buildings. Most country house builders organized the works themselves. They supplied both the plan and the materials, arranged the transport and then employed the workmen by the day. Occasionally, more skilled workmen were employed 'by measure' (also called 'prest' or 'task'), that is on piece work. For example, they might be asked to produce so many feet of decorative stonework, such as cornice, at so much per foot. The patron also had to bear in mind other practicalities like feeding and sometimes accommodating the workforce.

It is easy to see why the great landowners preferred to remain in control. They could often supply much of the building materials from their own estates or strike a deal with their neighbours for things they lacked, such as good building stone. Much of the unskilled labour could be drawn from their existing workforce. The ancient custom of fulfilling so many days work for the manor lord in part payment for tenancy, called boon work, was still in operation and provided some free labour. In an age when there was no protection for the workforce, there were benefits for the employer in using the day rate system. If work stopped for bad weather, or even because the builder had temporarily run out of funds or materials, the day labourers were simply laid off and their wages stopped immediately. Very skilled craftsmen were able to negotiate more secure conditions for themselves. Carpenters and stone carvers, for example, could carry on working inside when the weather was bad, preparing materials to be placed on site later. Sir Francis employed some of these 'by measure' and they could predict their future to a greater extent. Some, whose skills meant that they were in high demand, could hold out for an even better deal. In 1585 Sir Francis took on a skilled marble mason, a joiner, and a principal mason each with a whole year's contract, while two other masons remained on day wages but were paid £1 annual retention fee.

Over its eight years' duration the building of Wollaton Hall presented a massive logistical headache. The size of the workforce fluctuated not only from year to year but from month to month and even from day to day. There was a great variation in wage rates and an account had to be kept of who worked when and how much they should receive. The accounts suggest there were five clerks engaged in administering this. The need for materials also varied according to what stage the building had reached, and the failure to provide the necessary material at the right time could have resulted in delay. As 'architector-surveyor', Robert Smythson was not only instrumental in drawing up the overall plan, he was ultimately responsible for the smooth running of the whole business. Bearing in mind added problems like accommodating and feeding itinerant workmen, some of whom only came for short periods of time, this would have been a considerable enough responsibility, but there was more. Quality control would also have come under Smythson's aegis. Unsatisfactory workmanship or poor materials, even in one small section, would have undermined the whole building, for which he would have been called to account. Moreover, he would have been expected to introduce those particularly skilled craftsmen who could provide the embellishment of the house. Smythson had help on the accounting side from the gentlemen servants in Sir Francis's household, the notorious Ithel amongst them, and on the building side he occasionally gave the reins of supervision to a deputy master mason if he had to go away. Nevertheless, his roles were varied: he was expected to act as design consultant, head hunter, personnel manager, quantity surveyor, clerk of the works, accounts clerk supervisor, catering manager, wages officer and quality controller. His remuneration appears rarely in the surviving documents, and then only for specific isolated tasks or to reimburse him for expenditure laid out from his own pocket. It is assumed that for the most part Sir Francis paid Smythson directly for his services and it is impossible to tell how much he received.

Workers and Materials

Although the building accounts are at best incomplete and the disappearance of the records for the early work, carried out between 1580 and March 1582, is a particularly sad loss, they nevertheless represent one of the better documented building projects of the age. The recorded maximum number of workers engaged on the site at any one time was 76, although it also fell as low as 11 and there were some months when no work was done at all. When work was in progress, the number of people employed on site averaged around 35. The workforce fell into two main camps; the skilled craftsmen and unskilled workers, labourers and boys. Women were only very occasionally employed, but never as skilled workers. They helped with transport, collected limestone from 'the red field' for burning to make mortar and occasionally tended the lime kiln. The labourers quarried stone, dug sawpits and fetched and carried for the tradesmen, but in the first instance they must have moved a tremendous amount of stone and earth. The site chosen for the new hall was the summit of a hill, Camden describing it in 1600 as 'standing bleakly but offering a very good prospect to the beholders far and near'. The top of this sandstone hill was levelled to a flat surface and the sides were quarried away vertically so as to produce a huge rectangular base, like a massive stone altar. The basement rooms were constructed around the sides of this rectangular core, the floor level of each room rising and falling considerably according to the natural undulations of the ground, so that some basement rooms were twice as tall as others. The 'ground' floor was level with the top of the central stone core, so that the Great Hall in the very centre of the house sits on top of this base while the chambers which surround it sit on top of the basement rooms.

The labour involved in preparing the groundwork before construction even began must have been enormous, but the length of time and costs involved can only be guessed at. Much more excavation was needed prior to the construction of two long sewers which run underground, parallel to the east and west sides of the house (see chapter 9). These brick tunnels were then reburied and there might be a reference to this when 'Burrage and his fellows' were paid £1 19s 0d for levelling earth by the 'grund nich' (drain). There is a great deal more hidden brickwork within the house itself for, although the hall is encased in elaborately carved and moulded stone, this surrounds a brick interior shell. During 1584 and 1585 one William Hill supplied 189,000 bricks at 2s 3d the thousand and in 1588 an unspecified number were brought from Radford, the carriage costing 4d a load.

In the basement of the house all the walls are made of stone, but its provenance is not recorded. In 1990, however, an internal wall in a basement room was stripped and was found to be made of recycled stone from an early Romanesque church of some status. Without doubt, this had been recycled from neighbouring Lenton Priory. The small amount that has actually been uncovered in the hall is no doubt the tip of the iceberg and its presence probably explains why so little of the priory remains. On the exterior walls new stone was used. For courses up to and including the plinth, Mansfield stone was chosen as this fine-grained sandstone does not readily absorb moisture and acts as a sort of damp-course. Its source was quite local (14 miles away), and its colour blends well with Ancaster stone, which was chosen for the facades proper. This honey-coloured limestone was the best building stone in the region and was brought from Lincolnshire, a distance of 35 miles. The building accounts show that Smythson spent some time at the Ancaster quarry with the Wollaton masons, personally supervising the stone-getting. His efforts were worthwhile, for the stonework remains in very good condition and, except where openings have been altered and the work made good, the building has not been refaced. Cassandra stated that all the stone obtained at Ancaster was exchanged for coal and the people of Ancaster did the carrying. However, only one transaction where the commodities were swapped is actually recorded and this was probably an exception. In March 1583, for example, £98 8s 11d was paid for 'Bowght stone delyvered to Lovell and Roedes at the quarrey'. In contradiction of Cassandra's account, the cost of carrying is also recorded and this varied between 4d and 9d a load for the entire journey. The low price almost certainly shows that it was mostly done by boon workers.

The total recorded charges for timber used in the house amounted to £91 6s 9d, but two thirds of this was for sawing and carriage. It should be remembered that Sir Francis's own estates supplied most of the timber, although some was purchased as far away as Newbury. Some came from Sir Francis's Warwickshire manors but much of it came from West Hallam woods, where the felling of each tree cost 5d. The sawyers were paid 10d a day for 'breaking trees' (ie. trimming or squaring them), although sometimes this was put out to contract. In 1586, £4 18s 8d was paid to 'Okes and his fellows for breaking xliij trees in great' (ie. on contract), under 2s 4d per tree. The timber was transported in its rough-hewn state to the building site and, unless carried by boon workers, this cost between 2s and 2s 4d a load. On site, it had to be sawn into workable planks at a rate of between 8d and 1s 6d per hundred feet. This was a skilled job, but the preparation of saw pits was done by unskilled labourers and cost only 5d or 6d a pit.

A fair amount of iron was used in the building, not only for accessories such as hinges and locks, but often for iron bars placed at the windows for security. Some of it was used by the smiths working on the site to make tools. Much of the iron was supplied from Sir Francis's own works at Codnor in Derbyshire, from whence came 10 hundredweight of iron bars in one batch, costing 8d the hundredweight, a charge which relates to the carriage. Some was purchased from other works at the going price of 12s the hundredweight. Lead was purchased in huge quantities, not only for drainpipes and gutters, but for covering the roofs. It came from suppliers in Nottingham and Dale (Derbyshire) and cost 8s per hundredweight. The plumbers also required '22 strike of charcole for ye plomars to Fyne out lead of leade ashes' and the 'hyring a pare of bellowes to blowe the same'. They also needed tin to solder lead joints, twelve pounds of which was purchased for 5s 0d. Salt was used in the soldering process and also to guard against frost damage to the pipes. This was an expensive commodity, normally costing around 17s 4d a quarter, but only 4d is recorded for its purchase. Sir Francis probably had a cheaper source in Hull and the salt came down the Trent on his own barges along with household supplies like fish and wine.

Hundreds of thousands of nails were bought from four sources. Three of these were probably specialised nail-makers: Thomas Granger, William Naylor and Frythe of Eggerton. The fourth was a more general supplier of materials. Called, significantly, *Mr.* York, he also sold ironmongery, such as door bands and hinges, and ropes which were needed to lash the scaffold together and haul up the building materials. Specialist rope was bought for different purposes:

one hundred and eighty-six dozen scaffold ropes were bought at 10d the dozen, while two dozen ropes 'for to draw up tymber' cost 3s 4d. Cable ropes, also used for drawing heavy loads were even more expensive, at 7s 6d each. Other sundries included resin and wax which the masons sometimes put into the cement to make it weather better. Between 1586 and 1587, when most of the plastering was in progress, one hundred and ninety-nine stones of hair was purchased at between 4d and 8d a stone. This was added to the first rough or base coat to help it stick to the surface and ground alabaster was sometimes added to the finer top coats. Oyster shells were used in the fine joints between the stone courses to help achieve a level bedding and some of these are still visible in the joints.

Boon work helps to explain why the transport of materials was generally very cheap. Willoughby was owed boon work by the occupants of ten villages in Nottinghamshire and two in Warwickshire, Middleton and Kingsbury. Boon workers only seem to have been asked to load and carry materials, such as timber, limestone and brick. They provided their own teams of draught animals, usually oxen, and they could claim subsistence for themselves and their beasts. In 1587 men from the Warwickshire manors brought timber, claiming £1 1s 0d to sustain their eighty-nine 'beastes and horse' during their journeys of forty miles each way. In April of the same year an allowance of 3s 8d was made 'for bread and beere for carriage of x lode of Ankaster stone'. When engaged in this work, the Warwickshire men and those of the more distant Nottinghamshire villages of Willoughby and Bradmore had to stay away from home. They were sometimes accommodated by Mother Coton, who charged two rates for beds, one farthing and one penny. The rate possibly varied according to how many people had to share a bed. They were fed by Edward the caterer, who gave them veal, salt-fish, eggs, cheese and butter. Boon workers munched their way through £19 6s 0d worth of food during the recorded period of the building operation.

The Range of the Workforce

The labourers were paid on average 6d a day but women and boys got only 3d or 4d. The craftsmen were much better paid. Masons, carpenters, joiners and plumbers got a daily wage ranging from 10d to 14d while bricklayers and plasterers got slightly less, with a maximum rate of 10d and 12d per day respectively. Painters could earn 16d and apprentices got 7d or 8d a day. Other crafts included sawyers, glaziers and smiths. The workers had Sunday off and twenty-nine days unpaid holiday a year, although some of these were occasionally worked by labourers, who got an extra penny for the overtime; craftsmen never worked on Sundays or holidays. There was little machinery available to help the building process. The carpenters had a grindstone to sharpen their tools and there were pole lathes operated by cords for turning balusters. 'Twoe great gynes' are recorded, that is block and pulley cranes for raising heavy timbers or blocks of stone. Most of the tools were hand tools which were supplied for the unskilled workers, the craftsmen using their own. Aids laid on for the labourers included 'seves to seft lyme' as well as pails, scuttles, stoups and bowls. On one occasion the clerk paid 'Coton's wyf for the lone of a panne for ye plasterers at ye newe building for boyling of theyre syses [sizes]'.

The carpenters did the large-scale work in timber, like making floor-joists and roof members and they also arranged the scaffolding. Joiners did finer work in wood, such as making and fitting door-frames and panelling. They also might have made some furniture for the house, for there is a record of obtaining 'wallnutte trees for the drawinge tables'. The craftsmen whose skills were most prized were already known in their field and seem to have been recruited through personal contacts. The masons John Hills and Christopher Lovell came to Wollaton from Longleat, along with Richard Crispin, the head carpenter. Smythson is the obvious connection here and it was Lovell who acted as Smythson's deputy on occasion. Another mason, Thomas Accres, came to Wollaton from Chatsworth where he had been working for the Cavendishes: he was probably recommended to Sir Francis by Bess of Hardwick. When Wollaton was finished several of the craftsmen moved on to work at Hardwick

Ill. 12. Smythson's design drawing for the Hall screen. British Architectural Library, R.I.B.A., London [Smythson I/25(7)]

or later Worksop, both designed by Smythson. These men were able to negotiate their own terms for at least part of the time. The mason Lovell was taken on for the whole year in 1585 at a salary of £16 but Accres, who carved marble and was therefore perhaps creating elaborate fireplace surrounds, got a better contract at £30. Six tons of alabaster had been purchased in 1583 at a cost of 13s 4d a ton and Cassandra gives a description of one chimneypiece in the Dining Parlour 'which, adorned with a great deal of stone and alabaster carved, reached to the top of the room'. Unfortunately it had been badly damaged by fire when she saw it. Accres probably carved the Hall screen which is still there. The joiner Thomas Greenway also got a year's contract at £30 which perhaps suggests that he was engaged on some fine wood carving or panelling. Few interior details survive at Wollaton, but the outstanding quality of Accres' work can still be seen at Hardwick Hall in Derbyshire, along with much original woodwork of the period. The elaborate exterior decoration at Wollaton has survived its four centuries in excellent condition and most of this was done by 'measure' or piece rate. The mason Christopher Rhodes 'and his fellow' (assistant) were paid 'for base and shapiturs [capitals] for a tower at xxijd the pece'. They also produced 160 feet of architrave and frieze at 11d per foot and 521 feet of transoms and pilasters at 7d per foot.

Ill. 12 and 23

Ill. 13

Ill. 14

The plumbers were also essential workmen, for the hall was roofed entirely in lead. The vast area of almost flat roof space was actually called 'the leads'

Ill. 13. Chimneypiece and door surround in the Green Velvet Room at Hardwick Hall, Derbyshire executed by Thomas Accres in 1599. He was one of the more respected craftsmen who worked at Wollaton and his work at Hardwick gives some impression of what the Wollaton interiors might have been like. The wood panelling and door show the high quality of joinery at this period. © National Trust

Ill. 14. Detail of exterior decoration at Wollaton

Ill. 15

Ill. 16

and was used in the Elizabethan period for recreation. When paid by the day, plumbers got the top rate of 14d and their labourers could often get double the normal rate. Henry Wright was the chief plumber. He put in drainpipes, but his most important job was roofing, for which he was paid by measure at £1 per foot linear measurement.

The house was ready for plasterwork by the summer of 1586. Another skilled job, this was carried out by three men, Jepson, Raphael and Ragge, who seem to have been paid on piece rate. Jepson did mostly plain walling, getting £4 14s 6d for 509 yards of plain wall and 192 yards of 'latte and nail at 2d the yard'. He worked for a total of five months at the new hall, earning a total of £23 7s 10d and out of this he paid his own labourers but his materials were supplied. Raphael had worked at the quarry and as a layer, but turned to plastering over the winter of 1586-7. Ragge was clearly the most gifted of the three, undertaking the gallery ceiling, finished in June 1586, for £9. Sir Francis was so pleased with his plasterwork decoration in the Great Hall, that he gave him a bonus of £2.

The interior decoration got underway in August 1585, carried out by Mr. Matthews the Painter and his two assistants, Matthew Junior and Jackson. For much of their time they were engaged in painting window casements, at 4d each, and bars at 8d a dozen, although the tediousness of this was alleviated by occasionally 'drawing panel joints at 6d the dozen' and, in 1587 'blacking verses in the table on the garden side'. This meant applying paint to the carved letters of an inscription which commemorates the completion of the house, so that it would be easier to read from the ground. Perhaps Matthews' most fulfilling job was decorating two bed-chambers at the east end of the Hall, which were known thereafter as 'the painted chambers': their decoration cost £11 4s. 0d.

The glazing was undertaken by John Hyckynes, who first arranged for the supply of the window frames from John Beesley. Although Sir Francis's successor tried to set up a glassworks at Wollaton during the next century, there was no attempt to supply the extensive needs of the new house from a local source. The glass was supplied by a Coventry glass-maker and its transport must have been a nightmare. An estimate for glass in Smythson's hand, dated November 20th 1587, survives. It covers most of the house and estimated the cost at £50 9s 51/2d. A host of iron goods were needed to finish off the house, including 'latches, Katches and Hynges, Boltes and Staples and

Ill. 15. Details of plasterwork decoration in the Great Hall

Plate locke for the portall dores'. These were purchased ready-made from Mr. York, who had also supplied nails, raw iron and rope, and also from suppliers called Hazelhurst and Needham. Many of the heavy original hinges are still *in situ*, especially in the tower chambers.

Although the house was finished in 1588, work carried on in the grounds for some years. The extensive flat terrace on the south side where the formal gardens were laid out must have been artificially made up. There was probably some reinforcing grid pattern laid out in stone to stabilise the huge quantities of soil which were finally laid on top and it would also have required a long retaining wall. Since robbed or recycled stone was only used inside the house in places where it would not be visible, it is reasonable to suppose that it might have been used in the substructure of the landscaping operation and there is some documentary evidence to support this theory. In 1591, three years after the house itself had been finished, a book of extraordinary household expenditure records payments to Richard Gamble and his fellows for 'stonne-getting' at Lenton Priory and for carting it to the new house.

Ill. 16. An estimate for glass in Smythson's hand dated 20th November 1587.
By courtesy of the Hon. Michael Willoughby and Nottingham University Library.

Chapter 3: 'Willoughby's Glory': the finished house

Ill. 17. The south facade of the hall.

As far as we know, Wollaton Hall was the first building in which Smythson had a significant hand in the design rather than simply in the execution; at Longleat the plan was already in train and at Old Wardour he was essentially carrying out a conversion. In some respects Wollaton was architecturally innovative, yet in others it was rather conservative. One cannot help but suspect that Smythson did not have a totally free hand and that the finger of Sir Francis Willoughby was never far away.

The Exterior

It is the external appearance of the building which has aroused most interest, as well as criticism. The knight's extensive collection of architectural books, drawn from different parts of Europe, would have contained many patterns for decorative motifs and the external decoration of the new hall embraced many of these. It could be argued that it embraced too many. Cornices, pilasters, friezes, niches, cartouches, busts of classical worthies, elaborate Dutch gables and bartizans all vie with each other for attention, while the Renaissance lines of the fenestration employed on most of the house revert to late Gothic on the central tower. Influences from Jacques du Cerceau, Hieronymous Cock

Ills. 1. 14, 17 & 18

Ill. 19.

and Vredeman de Vries are all apparent, but the overall impression resembles a piece of confectionary and many critics have found it too overpowering. Was this excess due to Smythson's inexperience? If so, he adopted a very different approach to the exterior of Hardwick Hall, Derbyshire, his next major project. Here the lines are cleaner and the decoration much more restrained, any exuberance being restricted to the tower parapets which celebrate Elizabeth of Shrewsbury's initials. It is true that this restraint accentuates the vast expanses of glass used in the Hardwick facades, but one suspects that at Wollaton there was some anxiety on the part of Sir Francis that something stylish might be missed out, so that, to be on the safe side, virtually every available motif was put in.

Gardens and outbuildings

The ground floor plan of the house itself conforms pretty well with that drawn in Smythson's platt (Illus. 9). Although technically the house faces north-west, for the sake of simplicity it will be described as if it faces north. We cannot tell for certain whether the rest of the design, including the courtyards, gardens and outbuildings, all altered or completely swept away at a later date, was carried out to the full. There is always the possibility that Sir Francis's finances were becoming so strained towards the completion of the hall that some of the peripheral buildings were omitted. The chosen site also presented some problems in carrying out the plan exactly as drawn.

Ill. 18. Detail of the external decoration at Wollaton.

Ill. 19. The main facade of Hardwick Hall, Derbyshire. Built for the Countess of Shrewsbury, 'Bess of Hardwick'. Smythson designed this great house shortly after the completion of Wollaton. Photo © National Trust.

The decision to build the house on top of a hill might have maximised its visual impact, but the dramatic falling away of the land on each side except the east made it difficult to maintain the precise chequer-board design of the grounds implied by the drawing. The ground was made up artificially on the south side, enabling the scheme for the southern gardens to be followed closely. The circular feature shown in the centre probably represents the pond which still exists, for a drain was connected between the pond and the eastern sewer system, enabling it to be periodically emptied, and this appears to be an original arrangement. A labourer called Otewill was paid 2s 0d for 'pool-making', but whether this was for digging out the ornamental pool or for creating a cess pit is impossible to tell. The east side of the house, where the stables were to lie across a courtyard, was less of a problem, for the land was naturally flatter here. It was the north and west sides, where the ground falls away steeply and was not made up, that difficulties in adhering to the plan would have arisen. It is tempting to take documentary evidence relating to outbuildings at its face value, although there are some problems with such sources: one cannot be absolutely sure that they don't refer to outbuildings belonging to the Old Hall, which might have remained in use. However, in 1610 Thomas Ridgeway, the new father-in-law of Sir Francis's grandson, described Wollaton as a 'miracle, and true model indeed, of a most perfect and well-shaped house, none in England better, unless greater, and yet if this were greater it were the worser.' Significantly, he made a specific reference to 'the gatehouse, curtelages, gardens, orchards, stables, etc.' and a household inventory of 1609 also refers to bedding being delivered to 'the dairy house'.

There is, however, further evidence to suggest that the planned layout was followed as closely as possible. A fragment of ashlar walling in an underground ale cellar, added during the 17th century, possibly belonged originally to the colonnaded walkway flanking the entrance courtyard. The results of a geo-physical survey also suggest that a gatehouse was built, although this could only be confirmed by excavation. Developments on the west side of the house during the 17th and early 19th centuries also indicate that there was already a service courtyard there, as implied by Smythson's plan. This would be logical, for the service entries were located on this facade and it would be convenient to build the brew-house cum bakehouse close to them. On balance, it is likely that the hall and its immediate environs more or less followed the plan prepared by the architect. The undulations in the ground might have detracted somewhat from its grid-like form, but the benefits of raising the hall on its eminence were clearly considered to outweigh these.

Ill. 20.

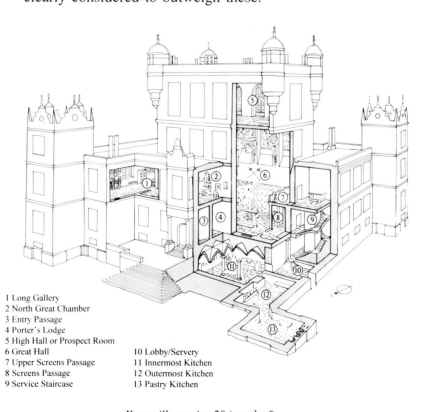

1 Long Gallery
2 North Great Chamber
3 Entry Passage
4 Porter's Lodge
5 High Hall or Prospect Room
6 Great Hall
7 Upper Screens Passage
8 Screens Passage
9 Service Staircase
10 Lobby/Servery
11 Innermost Kitchen
12 Outermost Kitchen
13 Pastry Kitchen

Key to illustration 20 (overleaf)

Ill. 20. *A cutaway reconstruction of Wollaton Hall in the 1590s. Drawing by David Taylor.*

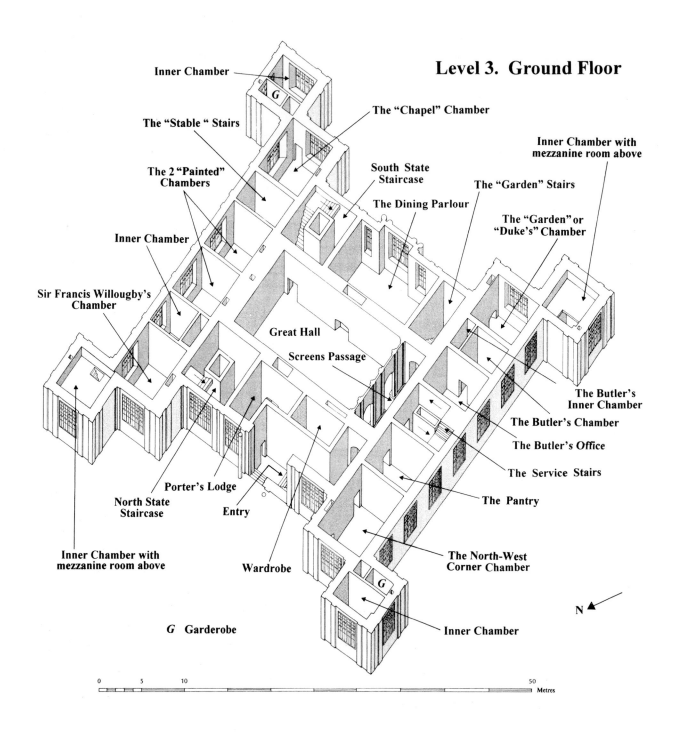

Level 3. Ground Floor

Inner Chamber

The "Chapel" Chamber

The "Stable " Stairs

Inner Chamber with mezzanine room above

The 2 "Painted" Chambers

South State Staircase

The "Garden" Stairs

The Dining Parlour

The "Garden" or "Duke's" Chamber

Inner Chamber

Sir Francis Willougby's Chamber

Great Hall

Screens Passage

The Butler's Inner Chamber

The Butler's Chamber

The Butler's Office

The Service Stairs

Porter's Lodge

The Pantry

North State Staircase

Entry

Wardrobe

The North-West Corner Chamber

Inner Chamber with mezzanine room above

Inner Chamber

G **Garderobe**

N

0   5   10   50
                                                          Metres

Ill. 21. *A bird's eye view of the ground floor as it would have appeared during the Elizabethan and Jacobean period.*
Drawing by David Taylor.

The Interior

The interior of the house was dominated by the Great Hall. It occupied the very centre of the house and was totally surrounded by other rooms on two floors. The flat roofs of these encircling wings, called the 'half-roof' or 'leads', provided walkways from which views of the surrounding countryside could be enjoyed. One would expect the Great Hall to be the equivalent of two stories in height, but because of the surrounding wings, in order to get any light at all, the Hall had to have an extra half storey added, rising above the surrounding wings to provide enough room for clerestory windows. At each corner of the house a tower rises to the level of the Great Hall clerestory and it is very likely that the house was originally planned to stand no taller than that. However, at some point before the building was finished it was decided to pile another hall, called the High Hall, on top of the Great Hall. This resulted in a huge central tower, with two tiers of windows, rising out of the centre of the building and it is this feature which makes Wollaton so distinctive. Little bartizan turrets overhang each corner and, combined with the surrounding corner towers, give the building a dramatic silhouette, the effect reminiscent of the outline of a medieval castle. The High Hall was not a particularly useful room, as we shall see, and the chief motive for adding it was probably to do with the visual impact it would add to the house when viewed from a distance.

The Main (Ground) Floor

Ill. 21.

The approaching visitor, having been suitably impressed by Wollaton's arresting skyline, then further dazzled by its external decoration, might have been a trifle disappointed on actually entering the building. Having mounted the steps of the north terrace and entered by the front door, they would have found themselves in a relatively restricted space, not at all the grand area they might have expected. Most of the available space was taken up by an L-shaped room where the porter lived and by a storage room called the Wardrobe, leaving a rather mean entrance lobby. However, they would turn right and, after climbing a short flight of steps, reach 'ground' floor level, in reality several feet above ground level outside. They then had a left hand turn before entering the Screens Passage of the Great Hall. Before them the Great Hall would reveal itself in all its glory, the hub of the household around which the whole building revolved.

The Great Hall

Apart from the twists and turns needed to get from the front door to the Hall, all of this was terribly traditional. The Hall had been the most important apartment in large houses since the Middle Ages. With its long side traditionally fronting the building, one entered straight into a cross-passage at one end of the hall: the front door was at one end of the passage and the back door was at the other. Smythson must have had a pretty game fitting this obsolete domestic arrangement into a square and perfectly symmetrical exterior based on the ideas of du Cerceau. The overall symmetry of the plan at Wollaton is actually ruined by the fact that the long side of the Hall faces the front of the building, causing the need to improvise the rather convoluted entry passage. It would have made more sense to turn the Hall through 90 degrees and enter at the short end, straight from the entrance vestibule. This is exactly what Smythson did at Hardwick. This arrangement allows the Hall to stretch out before the visitor, making an immediate impact, without treading corridors and making turns before reaching it. However, it meant sacrificing traditional domestic planning and perhaps Sir Francis was unwilling to depart from established custom. Even the traditional back door at the other end of the

Ill. 22. The Great Hall looking towards the screen. Note the false hammer beam roof. Photo by Philip Dixon.

screens passage was retained, for there was a postern doorway here, called 'the garden door' reached by descending a short flight of stairs. This led out into the south garden via a terrace.

The cross-passage in the medieval house was only created by erecting a screen, usually of timber, to divide it from the Hall. This screen went some way towards hiding the passage's other function, which was to provide a thoroughfare to and from the service rooms at mealtimes. Behind the screen, in the short end wall of the medieval hall, were three doors. One led to the buttery, where the ale was kept ready to serve, and another led to the pantry, where mealtime necessities were stored and which was regularly replenished with bread ready to be brought out. The middle door usually led outside into the yard, where the kitchen would be built separately because it was a notorious fire risk. Again, this arrangement was pretty old-fashioned by the 1580s, but was nevertheless followed closely at Wollaton. The Hall had its screen, though here executed in elaborately carved stone. One doorway led to the pantry and another to the butler's office. The central doorway did not lead out of doors, but nevertheless led to the kitchen, placed in the basement, via the service staircase. Sir Francis's Great Hall was designed to function in exactly the same time-honoured fashion as generations of medieval great halls before it. At Hardwick the screen was retained only as a vestige. On entering through the front door one passes through it to gain access to the Hall, but it had lost its

Ill. 22.

original function altogether.

The traditional approach at Wollaton did not end with the screens passage and the service doorways. Even the roof of the Hall took a medieval form, although this was largely cosmetic. The ceiling was set with pendant hammer beams, which served no structural purpose, made by a joiner called Gwillam for £28 10s 0d. Despite their plasterwork embellishment, executed by Ragge, these harked back to the previous century and were no doubt included because Sir Francis thought they would look 'right'.

In the later Middle Ages, a hall had a best or 'high' end, furthest away from the screen, where the master's table would be placed, and a 'low' end near the screen and services, where lesser members of the household would sit at mealtimes. Beyond the 'high' end of the hall, the master's private rooms were situated, often housed in a two-storey cross-wing attached to the end of the hall. These social niceties were also preserved in the Wollaton plan. Two doorways at the 'high' end of the Hall led to a row of good ground-floor bedrooms at the east end of the house, where Sir Francis and other family members slept. The doorways also led to the state staircases, by which one ascended to the Long Gallery and the best guest suites on the first floor.

Although it cannot be proved, the traditional approach which dominated the Wollaton main floor plan can most likely be attributed to Sir Francis's intervention. His building was designed to mark his 'arrival' in the top rank

Ill. 23. The Great Hall screen, carved by Thomas Accres. Photo by Chris Salisbury.

of English society and he perhaps felt that his house should reflect the accepted custom of countless generations. His dilemma was that on the one hand he wanted the latest architectural fashion, but on the other he was too conservative to abandon the old way of life. The result was an architectural compromise which Smythson, to his credit, managed better than might have been expected.

Daily life

As the upper floors contained the state, or special entertainment suites, the house was designed to function perfectly well using only the basement and ground floor. The Great Hall was used for communal meals involving the household at large, but the family ate in the more private 'Dining Parlour', with a large bay window facing the garden. This room was considerably altered in 1832 by the removal of the 'garden stairs' and it is now decorated in the style of the late Georgian period, so it is hard to imagine its Tudor form. It was originally a shorter room with a doorway at each end, one for 'polite' entry and the other for service or access to the garden. We know that a 'Joyner of Derby' was paid £13 for the wainscotting alone and that the magnificent fireplace of carved stone and alabaster reached from floor to ceiling. It was probably made by Thomas Accres, so we can be sure that the Dining Parlour was very impressively turned out.

Ill. 21.

Ill. 23.

The remaining ground floor rooms were good quality bed-chambers. Each of the jutting corner chambers was a bedroom, with a further *en suite* room in the adjoining towers. These 'inner chambers' were for personal attendants to sleep near their master or mistress. The inner chambers also had a garderobe (toilet) partitioned off in one corner. Two of the tower inner chambers, on the north-east and south-west corners, were divided horizontally into two floors, making a less lofty room in the lower half, but providing an additional mezzanine level room where more attendants could sleep. Where this occurred, it shows that the adjoining bedchambers were destined for more important occupants, who would have more personal servants.

Despite radical alterations, which were carried out in the house between 1801 and 1832, we can tell quite a lot about individual rooms during the Tudor and Stuart period from household inventories which list their contents. Sir Francis himself slept in the north-east chamber and when the Duke of York (the future Charles I) made a visit in 1604, he slept in 'the Chamber next the Garden Door'. The room was renamed 'the Duke's Chamber' after this visit. The bed was adorned with crimson velvet trimmed with silver cloth, while the window curtains were of yellow and blue taffeta. Other furniture included a square table and a Turkish carpet, probably draped over it. There was a blue velvet embroidered chair as well as stools covered in Turkish carpetwork and the walls were hung with county maps and 'a pedigree of the kings'. As well as implements to tend the fire, the apartment was furnished with a chamber pot. Two bedchambers at the east end of the house were known as the 'Painted Chambers'. They each had a garderobe but only the more northern of the two had an inner chamber. The southern Painted Chamber had to do without because its place was occupied by the 'stable' stairs.

The south-east corner chamber was called 'the Chapel Chamber', although it was always furnished and used as a bedroom, so the name is a mystery. There was no chapel inside Wollaton Hall, which was rather unusual. Sir Francis carried on living in the Old Hall even after the new one was finished and that had a well-furnished chapel, but this hardly explains why the new hall was left devoid of a place of worship. However, the years when the new hall was being built were politically very sensitive in terms of religion. England was moving towards war with Spain and the execution of the Catholic Mary Queen of Scots in 1587 brought this war to a head with the attempted invasion by the Spanish Armada in 1588, just as the house was being finished. There was just the hint of a Catholic skeleton in the Willoughby cupboard in the form of rumours about Sir Francis's great uncle John and in 1588 one of Sir Francis's business associates, Robert Payne, denounced him to the Privy Council for being in league with certain priests to aid the Spaniards. The accusation undoubtedly arose because their partnership was breaking down and nothing seems to have come of it. However, there was some talk of Willoughby being called before the Lord Chancellor, and it might have encouraged him to be extra careful about the possibility of private worship being misconstrued. Perhaps he considered it safer to worship publically in the parish church. It is possible that a chapel had been planned but abandoned, only the name lingering on in association with the chamber which took its place. However, no room identifiable as a chapel appears on Smythson's outline plan (Illus. 9).

Apart from the family and their special attendants, two officers of the household had rooms on the ground floor. The porter lived in his 'lodge' by the front door and the butler lived in a room behind his office. This room had started life as the Wardrobe, a storage space where household stuff was kept, but had been assigned to the butler by 1599, when the Wardrobe was moved next to the Porter's Lodge. The Butler's Chamber had a tiny inner chamber, about the size of a cupboard, situated over the passage entry to the Garden Chamber. It was reached by ladder and, despite its having no ventilation other than the door, one person slept in it. It must have been something of a privilege to have a room to sleep in at all, however cramped. Some of the servants would have been accommodated in the upper storeys of the outbuildings, the gatehouse, stables, bakehouse, brewhouse and dairyhouse, which were all drawn with staircases, but many more had no bedrooms. They slept in the public spaces of the main house, bringing out 'truckle beds' or simply mattresses at night. This meant that bedding had to be stored all over the place. Quite a lot was kept in the Wardrobe, and some was kept in cupboards in the central spaces

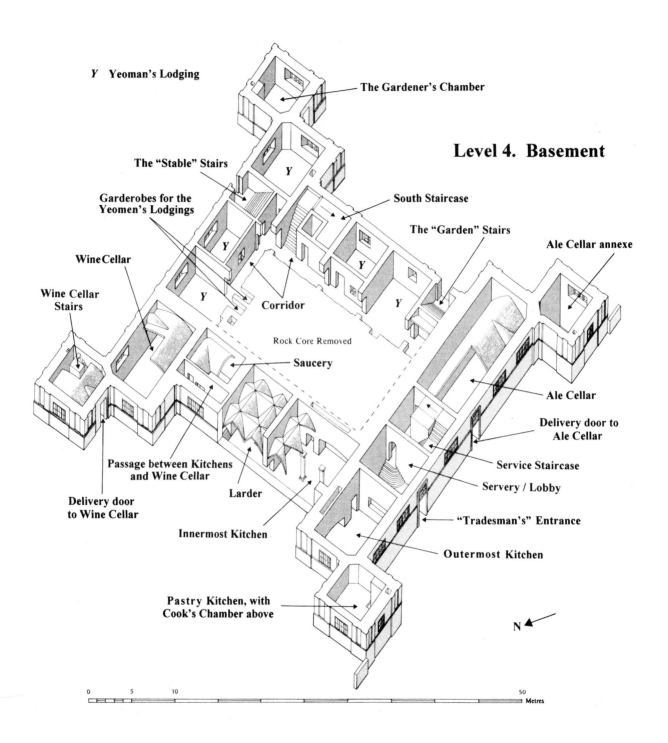

Y **Yeoman's Lodging**

The Gardener's Chamber

Level 4. Basement

The "Stable" Stairs

South Staircase

**Garderobes for the
Yeomen's Lodgings**

The "Garden" Stairs

Ale Cellar annexe

Wine Cellar

**Wine Cellar
Stairs**

Corridor

Rock Core Removed

Saucery

Ale Cellar

**Delivery door to
Ale Cellar**

Service Staircase

**Passage between Kitchens
and Wine Cellar**

Servery / Lobby

Larder

"Tradesman's" Entrance

**Delivery door
to Wine Cellar**

Innermost Kitchen

Outermost Kitchen

**Pastry Kitchen, with
Cook's Chamber above**

N

0   5   10   50
                                                                Metres

*Ill. 24. A bird's eye view of the basement as it would have beeen in the Elizabethan and Jacobean period.
Drawing by David Taylor.*

of the main staircases, which did not have open stair wells. Despite the grand interior decoration in the Dining Parlour, this room was used to store a fair amount of bedding. Its single 'livery cupboard' recorded in 1596 would have been hard pressed to hide away five featherbeds, one mattress, four bolsters, three pillows, six coverlets, four old blankets, four old quilts and 'an old greasie boulstere', all of which were also recorded as being kept there at the same date.

Life Below Stairs

Ill. 24.

Servants' Accommodation

The basement rooms, wrapped around the rock core upon which the Great Hall sits, were divided into two quite separate suites. One of these was solely to provide accommodation for the more privileged class of servants known as the 'yeomen', the household managers. It formed a massive 'L' shape around the south-east corner and was reached by the south state stairs, a mark of the occupants' status within the household, for the state stairs were for 'high' use only. It is also significant that, although these rooms shared the same floor as the services, there were very thick walls which kept them quite separate from the service area. The south staircase gave out on to a corridor which had to be lit by borrowed light from two of the rooms it served to reach. At the east end of this corridor, the room was large and it had a small inner room off it situated underneath the 'garden stair'. This had a strong barrel-vaulted roof to support the staircase. The inner room had no window but, given the pressure on sleeping space and bearing in mind the cupboard-like inner room off the Butler's Chamber, it might very well have provided an extra bedroom. The next main chamber was smaller, but also had an inner room underneath the main south staircase. In the south-east corner was a large room which had two windows and it was here that the robbed stones from Lenton Priory were found in the wall fabric. Underneath the 'stable stairs' was another small barrel-vaulted chamber which was lit by a borrowed light from the room next door. The occupants of these rooms all shared two lavatories at the top end of the eastern leg of the corridor, but the last chamber to be reached from this corridor almost certainly had its own. This and the other larger rooms might also have had their own fireplaces. An inventory of 1601 lists the contents of the 'Yeomen's Lodgings' and they all had standard equipment: '1 bedstide, 1 matte, 1 fetherbed and bolster, 1 old white rugge, 1 coverlett, 1 joined stool, 1 tressel borde'. The accommodation was well lit and ventilated and, compared with dragging mattresses on to the floor of the Great Hall or a corridor each night, pretty comfortable. The chamber at the base of the south-east tower, could not be reached from inside the house at all, but had a doorway directly into the garden. The 1601 inventory identifies it as the 'The Gardener's Chamber' and, apart from the standard furnishings, he kept in it '1 watering pott of brasse, 1 paire of garden sheares, 1 garden rake, 1 spaede, 1 garden lyne with iron prickes, 1 hande cutting hooke'.

Catering for the Household

Ill. 24.

The entire north and west wings of the basement were concerned with the serious business of furnishing the Wollaton tables. There were three doorways allowing access to services directly from outside the house, one to the wine cellar, another to the ale cellar and a third 'tradesman's entrance' into the lobby cum servery. The service staircase formed the link with the rest of the house. It was normal to cater for sixty people daily but when there were visitors the numbers would be far greater. As Knollys's letter to Willoughby on the subject of the Queen's aborted visit betrays, the 'holding out' of supplies could be a cause of considerable worry on special occasions, and Sir Francis was determined that if his new hall were graced with a royal visit, his household provision would not be found wanting. Two enormous vaulted cellars were built for storing drink. The wine cellar was in the north-east corner, beneath Sir Francis's own bedchamber. The barrels were brought in through a doorway in the north-east tower room, then rolled down a ramp into the cellar itself. The wine would be brought up to the high end of the Hall or to the Dining Parlour by a staircase in the north-east tower, a route which involved passing through Sir Francis's own bedroom, which must have become quite a thoroughfare at mealtimes.

The Ale Cellar was in the south-west corner and was even larger. There was a doorway leading directly into the western courtyard, across which the barrels were brought straight from the brew-house. The windows were kept deliberately narrow to help maintain a steady temperature, but they appear full width on the exterior so as not to detract from the overall symmetry of the facade. As the land on the south-west side of the house dropped considerably, the ale cellar floor was by far the lowest point of the basement. An additional staircase was needed at the north end of the cellar to link it with normal basement level, where the main service staircase began. On paper Smythson had planned that this staircase should link the cellar directly with the buttery on the ground floor, which would have made serving the ale to the Hall much easier. But when he came to build the hall he found this impossible to contrive because of the

Ill. 25. One of the pillars which supports the vault of the 'Innermost Kitchen'. The room has been used as a boiler-room since 1926. Photo by Philip Dixon.

terrain. However, this seems to be the only major difference between his executed and theoretical plan. The ale would join food being carried up the main service staircase and would enter the Hall, appropriately, at the lower end.

Food preparation took place in five rooms along the north wing. There were two main kitchens, the 'outermost kitchen' and 'the innermost kitchen'. Each had a very large fireplace for roasting, and the latter also had a small smoking chamber next to its fireplace for curing hams or fish. Each kitchen was well equipped with dressers and trestle tables, along with iron implements for tending the fire or cooking over it, including an 'iron gallow tree', bars and hooks. Bread would have been made in large quantities in the bakehouse attached to the brewhouse across the yard, but the more delicate baking of tarts and pies took place in the 'Pastry Kitchen' in the north-west tower room. The head cook lived above his work in a mezzanine level room over this.

Smythson originally planned that the 'Innermost Kitchen' should be much larger, five bays in length, with its extensive vaulted ceiling supported by a row of four columns. However this vault in turn had to support the walls of the Porter's Lodge, the entrance passage and the Wardrobe on the floor above. (This is best illustrated on Illus. 20, where no.11 is the kitchen, no.3 the entrance passage and no.4 the Porter's Lodge). The vault would no doubt have taken the superimposed weight, but Smythson was a cautious man and rather lost his nerve. Although he was content to let one of the dividing walls (that between the entrance passage and the Wardrobe) rest on the vault, he replaced one of the basement columns with a wall, right underneath the dividing wall between the Porter's Lodge and Wardrobe. This reduced the Innermost Kitchen to three bays and the remaining two were made into a Larder. Beyond this was a short passage connecting the kitchens with the Wine Cellar and, tucked to one side, was a small, vaulted room known as the Saucery, where the 'saucers' (saucepans) were kept. A household inventory of 1601 lists 'greate wood platters, washing tubs' and 'littl poudering tubbes' amongst its contents. It is unlikely that sauces were actually cooked here as there was no fireplace, but some preparation might have taken

Ill. 26. The western service staircase had to be wide enough for two-way traffic. The recess in the landing wall (right) is now blocked , but was an unglazed window from which an usher could call orders to the servery below. On the exterior facade the windows are as large as those elsewhere, although few window panes actually light the staircase. Where there was insufficient room for large openings on the interior, the overall symmetry was maintained externally by false windows. Photo by Philip Dixon.

place, and it was very handily placed next to the wine cellar for the enrichment of some of the more lavish sauces.

Serving the meals

When the food was ready to be carried upstairs, it would be taken to a hatch in the Outermost Kitchen wall. The servitors would gather in the Servery, which was also the Lobby to the 'tradesmen's entrance' of the house. The orchestration involved in getting the food, wine and ale up to the Hall and Dining Parlour at the right time, especially when there were several courses, was no easy task. As we have seen, the overall supervisor at meals was the gentleman usher, but it was no doubt intended that he should have assistants in the grand New Hall, particularly on special occasions. While the usher remained above stairs seeing that all ran smoothly in the dining apartments, he seems to have had two assistants, one at the top of the service stairs and another placed half-way down where, from an open, unglazed window he could survey the Servery from the half landing. The usher could indicate to the first fellow that a set of dishes or a quantity of ale were required and he would call the order on to the second. From his vantage point overlooking the whole Servery area, he was better placed to give specific orders to the servitors. At the base of the staircase, two very large niches were set into the wall, so that the waiters could set down heavy dishes, ready for the off as soon as they got the word. With waiters carrying food and ale upwards and spent dishes downwards, it was well that the staircase was made sufficiently wide for two-way traffic, but also a blessing that the wine waiters took a different route altogether. When special visitors were resident, as on the occasions of the royal visits in 1603 and 1604, the Great Chambers on the first floor would also have been used for dining. On these occasions there must have been a short string of 'callers' positioned on the stairs, while the waiters' legs must have felt the strain of climbing two stories with each dish.

Reception suites and entertaining areas

In the Tudor house the first floor was reserved for entertaining and occupation of the entire first floor would have been rare. The central space was taken up by the upper part of the Great Hall, which could be looked upon from windows on the landing of both the state staircases, as well as from the gallery over the screens passage.

Ill. 27.

The Long Gallery

The entire east wing was occupied by the Long Gallery, which measured thirty-seven metres in length. While the Long Gallery at Wollaton was divided

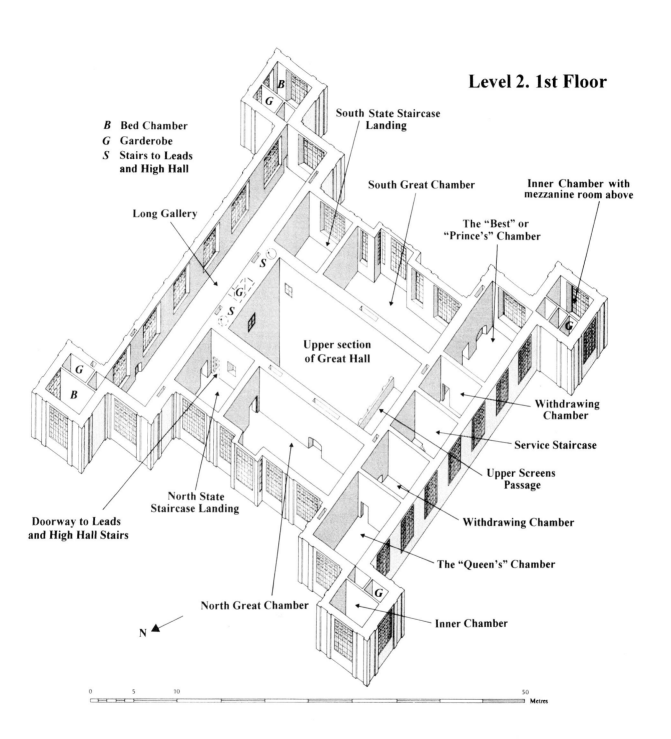

Level 2. 1st Floor

B Bed Chamber
G Garderobe
S Stairs to Leads and High Hall

South State Staircase Landing

South Great Chamber

Inner Chamber with mezzanine room above

The "Best" or "Prince's" Chamber

Long Gallery

S

Upper section of Great Hall

G

S

G

B

Withdrawing Chamber

Service Staircase

Upper Screens Passage

Withdrawing Chamber

North State Staircase Landing

Doorway to Leads and High Hall Stairs

The "Queen's" Chamber

G

North Great Chamber

N

Inner Chamber

0   5   10   50   Metres

Ill. 27. A bird's-eye view of the first floor during the Elizabethan and Jacobean periods.
Drawing by David Taylor.

Ill. 28. The long gallery at Hardwick Hall. This immensely impressive Elizabethan room gives us some idea of what the gallery at Wollaton would have looked like. Photo by G. Challifour, © National Trust

into smaller rooms during the early 19th century and its ceiling lowered, the gallery at Hardwick Hall gives us a good impression of what the one at Wollaton would have been like. Both were heated by two large fireplaces, placed one at either end. One could reach the Wollaton Gallery by either of the state staircases and it is likely that, of all the first floor rooms, this was the only one that was used regularly. In Elizabethan houses galleries were used to take gentle indoor exercise; to walk up and down while conversing and admiring the family portraits and other treasures displayed there. At one of the windows the Willoughby arms were worked in stained glass and Sir Francis also exhibited his family pedigree in this room. During the 16th century there was a great interest in owning maps, which were still quite rare and expensive, and there were no less than nine on show.

Ill. 28.

There was a garderobe off the Long Gallery which took borrowed light from the Great Hall. Its window, placed high up and now covered by a clock, must have given a very good view of proceedings in the Hall. At either end of the Long Gallery there was a tower chamber, which seem to have been used as bedrooms. The northern chamber is mentioned twice in the household inventories (in 1601 and 1609) and was better furnished than other tower chambers. It appears to have been unique amongst them in being heated, for a fire iron grate is listed in its contents and the north-east tower is the only one with an original flue.

Ill. 29.This walnut cupboard at Hardwick Hall, based on a design of c.1560 by du Cerceau, gives some impression of what the furnishings at Wollaton would have been like. Photo by G. Sweetman, © National Trust.

The State Suites

The rest of the first floor was divided into two suites of twin apartments, facing north and south respectively. They were practically a mirror image of one another, although the southern suite had slight refinements which show it was the superior of the two. This duplication of sets of rooms so that the owner could accommodate a guest, along with his or her retainers, whilst housing himself in a similar fashion, has good medieval precedents. The spaces allocated to each were more or less equal, both in terms of size and comfort, so that protocol was not breached by one having to suffer less dignity than the other. Each could maintain their privacy, yet meet and socialise when appropriate.

Each suite contained the necessary accommodation for formal living. The main room was a Great Chamber with its principal entrance from a state staircase. Each Great Chamber would be used for select dining and entertaining, so it required a service doorway as well. This was at the other end of the room, where it came directly from the gallery over the screens passage. The servants bringing items from the kitchens would use the service stairs, as usual, but continue up to the first floor, where the gallery over the screens acted as an upper screens passage. Each of the Great Chambers had a wall virtually full of glass, although the effect of this was destroyed during the Georgian period, when many of the windows were made narrower. The South Chamber was distinguished by a wider bay window and also by its view over the formal garden and park beyond. It was furnished with a pair of dining tables with forms and chairs covered in black or red leather or embroidery. There were many stools upholstered in silk or 'Turkey' carpetwork, two 'drawing' or occasional tables and a 'livery cupboard' for storage. There were several cushions covered in tapestry or needlework and, as well as ironmongery for tending the fire, a pewter 'cistern'. On the walls hung maps of Europe, the Low Countries and Jerusalem and a pedigree of Christ. It is possible that Sir Francis ran out of money before he was able to furnish the north Great Chamber adequately. All that is recorded there before his death in 1596 is 'various pieces', which is rather vague. By October 1599 the family had hung the room with six tapestries. In 1601, only two years before a visit by Anne of Denmark, James I's queen, and her son, Prince Henry, the only piece of furniture in the room was one drawing table. The chamber had probably been furnished in time for the distinguished guests, but remained relatively spartan, with only a dining table and two forms, a cupboard, a stool and another, smaller, table recorded in 1609.

Beyond the Great Chambers lay the state bed-chambers. The northern bed-chamber is called the 'Queen's Chamber' in the inventory of 1609, no doubt recalling the visit of Queen Anne in 1603. It was hung with a tapestry and the bed had a tester and valance of red and green velvet. The southern bed-chamber was much more grandly furnished and is identified by earlier inventories as the 'Best Chamber', but by the inventory of 1609 as the 'Prince's Chamber'. Price Henry, who was heir to the throne, would have been honoured with the best bed-chamber in the house when he accompanied his mother. The tester and valance on the bed were of crimson damask embellished with gold lace and embroidered with arms, while the hangings were of red taffeta and the coverlet was of flesh-coloured silk lined with red. There was a suite of one chair and two stools upholstered in purple velvet (or blue, according to another inventory-taker with a slightly different colour sense). There was another chair covered in needlework and two stools covered in 'tufted taffeta'. The window curtains were blue and there was a Turkish carpet, probably laid over a livery cupboard rather than lying on the floor, where there was a mat. Five maps hung on the walls.

As with the downstairs bedrooms, each of the state bed-chambers had an inner chamber, complete with garderobe, in the adjacent tower. The 1601 inventory speaks of a second (mezzanine) chamber over the inner chamber to the best chamber, as one would expect for the extra servants attending an important person. The state suites also each had a small withdrawing chamber where the furnishings were less lavish, but still reasonably well-appointed. These were probably intended for the use of high-ranking attendants.

Roof level: recreation areas on 'the leads'

The whole of the roof area formed part of a recreational complex. The roofs of the wings surrounding the central tower, called the 'half roof' or 'the leads' were used to enjoy the views and take some exercise in the open air, a sort of long gallery out-of-doors. A garderobe was even provided. At each corner of the house the turrets were crowned with pavilions which were originally reached only from the leads, although they now have internal staircases which date only from the 19th century. The north-east turret had a flue serving the room off the Long Gallery so, theoretically, the north-east pavilion could also have had a fireplace. None of the other tower rooms was heated until the 19th century. Like four of the turrets on the roof at Longleat, these pavilions were intended for intimate 'banquets' or picnics during the summer months. After dinner, small parties would retreat to them to enjoy the views, listen to music

Ill. 30.

Ill. 31.

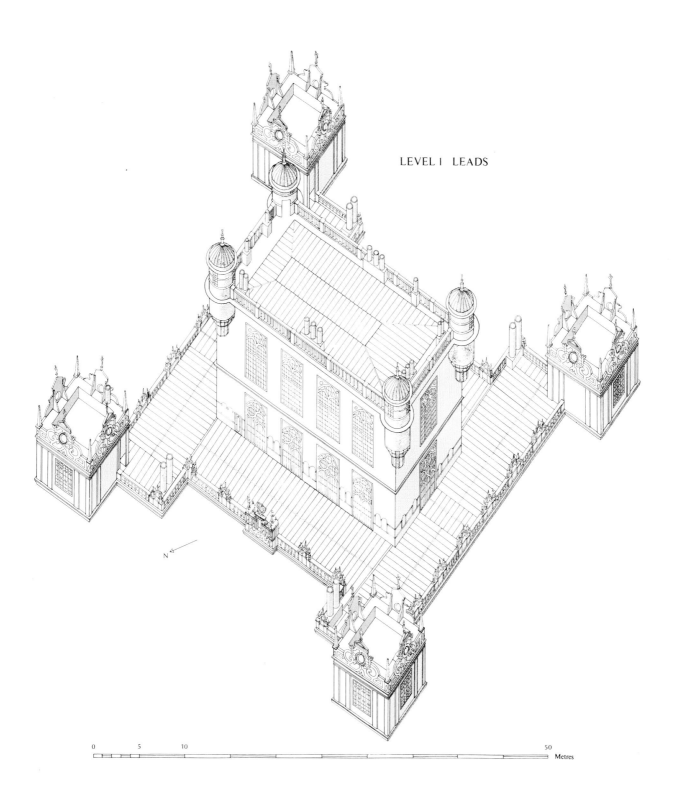

LEVEL I LEADS

N

0   5   10   50
Metres

Ill. 30. *A bird's-eye view of the 'Leads' of the Elizabethan house (Drawing by David Taylor)*

and indulge in witty conversation. They would eat fruits and sweetmeats and also continue drinking. 'Banqueting' parties got quite a bad reputation for immoral behaviour during the late Tudor period. Catering must have been simple in view of the distance from the kitchens and the awkwardness of the access. The earlier inventories do not include the turret chambers at all, and the later ones, of 1601 and 1609, show them to contain bedding. As we have seen, multiple use of rooms was common and it would be expected that the pavilions would also be used as sleeping accommodation, but perhaps less frequently. Their inconvenient access across the open leads and their sole convenience (a garderobe in the thickness of the central tower east wall), suggest that they would be assigned to servants, perhaps the retinue of visitors when the house was full.

Ill. 32.

The leads were reached by two narrow spiral staircases off the landings of the state stairs. They were lit by borrowed light from the Great Hall through small loop windows. Half way up, a doorway gave out on to the half roof and the pavilions, but the stairs continued upwards to reach the High Hall and, beyond that, the roof of the central tower. The first leg of the northern spiral staircase was blocked during the 17th century, when its doorway on the landing of the north state staircase was removed to accommodate a large mural painting, but it is still accessible from the half roof upwards. The well-finished balustrades at the very top of these stairs show that they were not merely meant to be seen and used by artisans carrying out repairs, but that the family and their guests ascended to the tower roof to appreciate the views. The stairs culminate in 'types', small circular domed chambers which project from each of the four corners of the tower. They imitate late medieval bartizans, turrets originally devised as defensive features but which, like these at Wollaton, soon became primarily decorative.

Ill. 31. One of the turret pavilions

Ill. 32. The staircase to the leads and the 'High Hall'. Negotiating these stairs in a farthingale could not have been easy.

Ill. 33. The interior of the High Hall as it appears today. The decoration belongs to the Georgian period, with trompe l'oeil drapery painted on boards at the windows. The modern steel braces are necessary to prevent outward movement of the central tower walls.

The High Hall or Prospect Room

Ill. 33.

The High Hall, later called the Prospect Room, is one of Wollaton's most striking features. Sitting on top of the Great Hall (see illustration 20), it adds considerably to the imposing appearance of the building, but in practical terms was almost useless. It was never heated, so could only have been used for half the year, and its restricted access meant that servants could not easily have brought refreshments there. It was certainly never designed to act as an additional great hall. Its furnishings were very sparse: its sole appearance in the household inventories records 'certain mats and a joint stool' in 1601. It seems to have been conceived, as its later name implies, as a room to walk in and admire the view while being sheltered from the weather, and it is correspondingly well furnished with large windows.

Ill. 34.

The theory that the High Hall might have been an afterthought and not originally intended is supported by a structural weakness in its design which is alien to the cautious practice Smythson displayed everywhere else in the building. It has been mentioned that the hammer beam roof of the Great Hall is cosmetic rather than structural. The Great Hall roof is actually formed by an inter-linking structure made up of main joists which were quite short, a system known as the 'Chinese Lattice' method. It was featured in the Italian architect Serlio's influential book *Architecture,* published in 1566 and was perhaps devised as an answer to an increasing shortage in western Europe of good long timbers. This motive might have prompted its adoption at Wollaton, although Sir Francis was clearly fascinated by architectural works and might have been attracted to the idea of trying out this novel technique. Despite his entrenched conservatism when it came to the practicalities of day to day living, he displayed an intellectual interest in building and it might have appealed

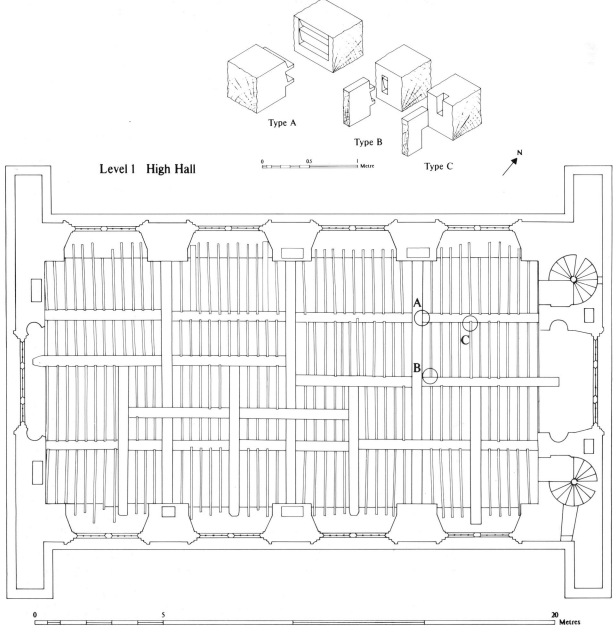

Ill. 34. A plan of the joist arrangement which acts as the roof of the Great Hall and the floor of the High Hall. Drawing by David Taylor

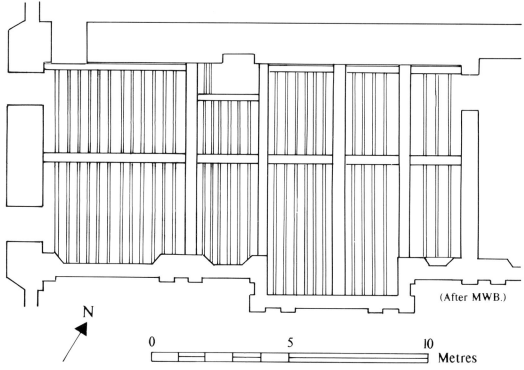

(After MWB.)

N

0   5   10
Metres

Ill. 35. A conventional arrangement of joists was used in the floor of the South Great Chamber, where the distance to be spanned was much narrower than that of the High Hall. A similar system would have proved stronger for the Prospect Room floor, but timber was becoming more difficult to obtain during the latter part of the 16th century and this was probably a factor in opting for the use of the Chinese Lattice method there. Drawn by David Taylor after M.W.Barley.

to him. Whatever the reason, the method was used to span the distance of almost ten metres which separated the long walls of the Hall. Not one joist reached from wall to wall to act as a tie but, part way across the span, a joist would be jointed into another running at right angles. A conventional tie-beam, stretching from wall to wall, would have helped to counter any outward pressure placed on the walls but, with the lattice arrangement, such pressure would tend to pull the joints apart. The system might have held if the roof of the central tower had been placed directly over the Great Hall, as Smythson might have intended, for the pressure would have been less. Piling the High Hall on top raised the walls of the central tower to such a height that their outward thrust was bound to strain the Chinese Lattice structure to the limit. Nevertheless, the High Hall went ahead. Whether it was a last minute idea we shall never know, for the records reveal nothing specific on the subject. We cannot even be sure that Smythson was able to foresee the weakness that would be caused in his building. We can only guess that, judging from the architect's normal wariness, he might have been unhappy with the scheme but was unable to deflect his determined patron. Within a century the central tower walls were pushing outwards and, despite various measures taken over time to redress the problem, the Chinese Lattice, which forms the floor of the Prospect Room, was considered unsafe by 1832 and the room has been unusable ever since.

Chapter 4: Family and Finance

'Money grows every day scantier.....'

Cassandra Willoughby stated that she saw a building account in the Wollaton library which put the total cost of the new hall at £80,000. Cassandra was not entirely accurate in other claims that she made regarding the new building, for example in asserting that the master workmen came from Italy and that all the Ancaster stone was acquired in exchange for coal. The surviving building accounts show that neither of these were true, and she was equally adrift in her estimate of the cost. It is possible that, while taking her notes, she inadvertently added an extra nought to her transcription, for the figure of £8,000 accords well with the surviving documentary evidence for the final cost of the house. Even so, this was an enormous sum, for the modern equivalent would approach eight million pounds in real terms. There is no evidence that Sir Francis made any special arrangements to meet these extra charges of £1,000 a year during the period of the building operation. When he embarked on the project the annual profits from his coal pits alone would have been sufficient to finance the scheme, so he probably thought he could meet the charges out of income. He was mistaken. Coal revenues were falling, as was the real value of rents, while inflation was rising. The marriages of three of his daughters, Bridget, Dorothy and Margaret, were to stretch his resources a little during the course of the building period and in 1582 he was forced to provide his wife with £200 a year for separate maintenance. Sir Francis took out his first loan of £300 in 1581, another of £500 following close behind, each at 10% interest. Between 1583-85 his outgoings amounted to at least £13,000, possibly more, and he showed no sign of curtailing his taste for good living. During the same period he borrowed £5,656, his debts compounded by the extortionate rates of interest current at the time. Further borrowings followed and by 1589 his indebtedness amounted to almost £12,000, at a time when it was said that 'money grows every day scantier than other, and those that have money stick not to ask twenty in the hundred for it, and such are men's wants that rather than they will go without it they daily give it.'

Sir Francis's problems might have been solved at an early stage if he had raised capital by parting with some land, but he seems to have been particularly unwilling to follow this course. Although he did sell parcels of land, he bought more to replace the loss, despite the fact that income from rents at the time was insufficient to clear his financial problems. During the 1580s he looked to entrepreneurial schemes to bring about financial salvation. First he went into partnership with Robert Payne, the author of an essay on the growing and processing of woad, a plant which produces a blue dye for the textile industry. He was following something of a trend, for the decade saw such a rise in the adoption of this crop that eventually the government took steps to discourage its production. The queen herself issued a request that it should not be grown near routes she was likely to take on progress because its rank smell when ripe was so disgusting. Willoughby had 40 acres planted in 1585 and he also had a hand in setting up a plantation in Ireland. The enterprise failed to prosper and Payne ended up in prison. It was he who brought the allegations that Sir Francis was in league with the Spaniards in 1588; hardly a reliable or unbiased witness.

Towards the end of the decade Sir Francis turned his attention towards iron production, borrowing heavily to invest in blast furnaces at Middleton, and also at Oakamoor in Staffordshire and Codnor in Derbyshire. Again, Willoughby had a business associate, Laurence Loggin, who, in theory, provided the technical expertise while he raised the capital. Again, the ventures failed to come up with the expected results. At one stage production at Middleton was halted for lack of funds to operate the works. Oakamoor was on land belonging to Bess of Hardwick whose woods provided fuel for the furnaces, at a price. She lent Willoughby the capital, £400 at 10% interest, and he mortgaged some of his Wollaton land to her. Even so, the works could not be built for another two years, during which time the interest was mounting. At Codnor, Sir Francis entered into business with his neighbour, Sir John Zouche, a man who was so deeply in debt that his credit rating was already nil. Nevertheless, Sir Francis borrowed £2,500 to lend him. His assurances that the two of them were pure gentlemen, who would never behave like 'griping merchants or cut-throat brokers' counted for little when the whole matter ended up with the usual acrimonious court case. Eventually his ironworks went into profit, but too late to extricate Sir Francis from the financial mire into which he was already all but submerged.

Family Matters

In the meantime, matters within the family had not stood still. When Sir Francis separated from his wife in 1579, Elizabeth kept custody of their only son, an infant who died the following year. The loss of this last hope of a male successor must have hit Willoughby very hard. Lady Willoughby was equally distressed and her health was as poor as ever. Having had a cooling off period, she also found the life of a separated woman hard going and wrote to Sir Francis to propose a reconciliation. She pointed out that she was already over forty and would soon be past child-bearing, but affirmed that she was prepared to do her best to fulfil his hopes of a healthy male heir: 'though she could not expect it without hazarding her life, yet she would contentedly run that hazard, with the hopes to establish the house of the Willoughbys'. The loss of his son and the continuation of his line no doubt weighed heavily on Sir Francis's mind and he must have given serious consideration to his wife's proposal. At last, however, on facing the prospect of Elizabeth's return, he decided that a grandson would do nicely and resolved to arrange a marriage for his eldest daughter.

Percival, the chosen bridegroom, could hardly have been more suitable to act as the surrogate provider of a Willoughby heir: he was a second cousin of Sir Francis and they shared the same surname. Willoughby's aunt Dorothy, his father's sister, had married Sir Robert Willoughby of Bore Place in Kent. Although they had the same name, they were not related: Robert descended from the Willoughby's of Eresby in Lincolnshire. It was their grandson, Percival, who was now selected to marry Bridget. Her dowry of 2,000 marks (about £1,330, worth just over one year's expenses for the Willoughby household) was quite small considering the status of the family. No doubt this reflected the expectation that she stood to inherit the bulk of the estate, but Sir Francis was unwilling to commit his entire fortune to his ostensible heiress. The manors of Wollaton with Sutton Passeys, Cossall and Trowell in Nottinghamshire and those of Middleton and Kingsbury in Warwickshire were to fall to Percival and Bridget in default of Sir Francis producing a male heir, but his remaining manors and interests were kept deliberately unattributed, to be used as a ploy to keep his children in line. Percival and Bridget's position was insecure. As Sir Francis was only in his mid-thirties and his estranged wife's health had always been poor, there was always the possibility of his being widowed, remarrying, and fathering a second brood.

Ill. 3.

Ills. 36 & 37.

Ill. 36. Percival Willoughby (1554-1643).
Portrait by courtesy of Hon. Michael Willoughby.

Ill. 37. Bridget Willoughby (c.1566-1629).
Portrait by courtesy of Hon. Michael Willoughby.

The marriage of Bridget and Percival

Cassandra informs us that Bridget and Percival's wedding took place in December 1580, and is very precise on the details of the arrangements. On November 2nd Willoughby set out for London with ten servants, the journey lasting six days. He set up house at Lincoln's Inn Grange and entertained until the end of the month, inviting between thirty and fifty guests each evening. On November 30th he travelled into Kent to attend the wedding. £156 18s 9d was spent on clothes for the bride, which did not include 10s for a tailor who had to travel into Kent three times to 'mend the gown'. Immediate wedding expenses exceeded £500, excluding tips to household officers. Sir Francis must have cut quite a figure as he progressed to his daughter's wedding with a rather noisy retinue, for 'the trumpeter going into Kent' was paid 6s 8d, as was a herald. At Bore Place, the bridegroom's home, the butler and cellarman were each tipped 6s, while the cook got 10s, the chamberlain 4s, the pantler and usher of the hall 3s each and 'the servant that helped to dress the horse' 1s. Willoughby spent a week at Bore Place and another week in London, with more lavish entertainment, before returning to Nottinghamshire. The cost of the wedding probably exceeded £1,000, almost as much as the dowry, bearing in mind the expenses of the journey and Willoughby's entertaining while he was resident in the capital.

Despite the arranged nature of the marriage, Percival and Bridget were to form an affection for each other which lasted throughout their lives. He went abroad alone shortly after the marriage perhaps, as Cassandra assumed, for health reasons, but more likely to broaden his mind and to allow his young bride some time to mature, a common practice. He was twenty-six but Bridget was over ten years his junior. Their own son spent the first three years eight months of his marriage away from his eleven-year-old bride. During their separation Percival's letters to Bridget were filled with expressions of devotion, occasionally extending to a poem or the drawing of a heart pierced by arrows. By contrast, relations between Sir Francis and Lady Elizabeth were apparently as bad as ever. Before the wedding, Percival wrote to Bridget expressing his hope that she might be allowed to come to him in London: 'I have used all means possible for your coming to town, but can't prevail. Your father doubts if you were here you would either see your mother, or your mother see you, which he in no case would [allow] .....'. When Bridget was settled in her in-laws' house after the wedding, Willoughby wrote to her with predictable advice on being a dutiful wife: 'for 'tis not beauty nor fortune but good qualities and a virtuous disposition which makes a gentlewoman esteemed....', adding that 'she will learn by others ..... (she may guess who he means) to be wise and not repent too late.' Bridget continued to please her father by steering clear of her mother. Cassandra quotes a letter from Lady Willoughby in reply to her son-in-law's excuses for Bridget's not going to visit her. In May 1584 she wrote that: 'she does not think him answerable to his wife's faults, and that if in forgetting her duty to see her she contented any other [ie. Sir Francis], it was well done, and she was content to make a virtue of necessity, trusting hereafter to have more comfort of her'.

More Division

In 1584 the new house at Wollaton was under construction and the family still lived in the Old Hall. Percival, back from his travels, and Bridget joined Sir Francis's household for at least part of the year. This situation did not, apparently, suit Sir Francis's servants who, having seen off their mistress, now began to regard Percival as a threat to their supremacy. Their reputation was such that Percival's father, Sir Thomas Willoughby, wrote to his son in April 1584, advising him to be careful how he meddled in their differences. They soon began to employ their old methods to bring about Percival's downfall. Cassandra assessed the situation succinctly as follows: 'Sir Francis's servants had very little regard to the interest of their master or his family, but made it their chief care to enrich themselves, which, I believe, they found more easy for them to do when Sir Francis lived by himself than when his lady or any of his children lived with him.' The happy and even course of Percival and Bridget's marriage was therefore subjected to all the rigours the servants could impose, but survived intact.

The initial problem arose because Percival brought with him a French servant called Francis Conrados, whom he had picked up in Lyons to teach him Italian. The demeanour of this man, 'a very proud, haughty person' who 'carried himself very insolently', immediately offended the other servants, but their noses were further put out of joint when they thought he was to have preferential treatment. Not only did Percival request that Conrados should eat at his own table, but he asked to have him installed in Marmion's bedroom. We have seen how scarce private rooms were in the new house, and there is no reason to suppose that the situation was any better in the old one. The allocation of rooms must have caused continual wrangling, especially as a good room was seen as a mark of rank and favour. Marmion wouldn't budge, but Cludde, whom Lady Willoughby had accused of drawing a sword on her at Kingsbury, was apparently displaced instead. Such ructions were caused that Percival began to regret he had ever set eyes on Conrados. Deciding that discretion was the better part of valour, he dismissed the Frenchman, but this only compounded his difficulties. Marmion, Cludde and two other servants called Blyth and Markham now saw how they could enlist the disgruntled Conrados to form a conspiracy even more damaging to Percival. They got Conrados to write a letter to his master, not only upbraiding him for his dismissal, but also making reference to other, imaginary misdemeanours which were proof of Percival's bad character. The most serious of these concerned 'many disrespectful words which he [i.e. Percival] had spoken of Sir Francis, and that he had threatened that if he could but get Sir Francis Willoughby's estate made secure to himself, Sir Francis should not live long after'. Needless to say, on its way to Percival this letter fell into the hands of Sir Francis himself, who fell for the ploy completely. His reaction can well be imagined.

Percival was distraught at being 'framed', but was powerless to persuade Willoughby of his innocence. Thomas Markham made sure that the affair got a wider audience by distributing copies of the infamous letter. It was said that he had an additional grudge against Sir Francis because he refused to let one of his younger daughters marry Markhams' son. Lady Willoughby, then living in Hoxton, Middlesex, got a copy and practiced her idea of discretion: 'who, for the goodwill she bears [Sir Thomas Willoughby, Percival's father] will suffer nobody to have a copy of it, but reads the letter herself to all that come to her.' Relationships within Sir Francis's household were as stormy as ever: at one stage Percival drew his sword on Markham outside the Lord Chancellor's house and his father and cousin had to visit the Lord Chancellor to smooth things over. In the end, Conrados approached Sir Thomas, offering to tell all and clear Percival's name for the sum of £40: the knight told him 'he should have such reward as his villainy deserved.' But the damage had been done. Sir Francis was never fully reconciled to Percival and, thanks partly to the efforts of Lady Willoughby, his family name had been the subject of gossip once again.

Public harmony, private discord

For a few brief years there were outward signs that discord in Willoughby's household had abated and things were going better. Sir Francis could not afford to remain estranged from Percival and his father for too long because they were enmeshed together in a web of debt. According to Cassandra, Willoughby 'often employed Sir Percival and Mr. Thomas Willoughby, his father, to borrow money for him and to be bound with him for it.'

In June 1587 Sir Francis's second daughter, Dorothy, married Henry Hastings, the Earl of Huntingdon's nephew. Willoughby excused himself 'for not keeping their wedding at his house, nor desiring that the young couple should stay with him till Michaelmas because, by reason of his wife's absence and the furniture of his house being much decayed, he had not designed to keep house this year'. The practical Cassandra adds that 'Wollaton new house was not finished till the year after this, and it is likely that Sir F[rancis] Willoughby did not care to buy any new furniture till he went into that house'. His domestic circumstances did not prevent him from entertaining Sir Thomas Stanhope that month at the New Hall, which was approaching completion. Sir Francis's third daughter, Margaret, was married to Robert Spencer of Wormleighton in Warwickshire the same summer and in November 1587, Willoughby felt able to lay on a dinner for one hundred and twenty people at the new house, the guests including the local noble and gentry families.

Willoughby's social standing was improving. His name appeared on a list of persons considered suitable for elevation to the peerage compiled by Lord Burghley, the Queen's chief minister, although the suggestion was not acted upon. He was reconciled with his wife in 1588, although the reasons behind this remain obscure. We know that in the mid 1580s Sir Francis was discouraging his offspring from having any truck with their mother and that in 1585 there were rumours that he would seek a divorce on the grounds of Lady Willoughby's adultery, a charge she fervently denied. However, Lady Willoughby had never left off her entreaties for *rapprochement* and had tried to enlist Percival to her cause. She had more success with his father, for in 1585 Sir Thomas wrote that 'Sir Francis Willoughby's lady and he are grown to great friends, and that she opens all her griefs to him, of Marmion, Cludde, etc.' The Spencers, Margaret's husband and father-in-law, had also become friendly with Elizabeth and were working towards a reconciliation. These ambassadors clearly had some effect, but the pursuit of improved public relations might also have been a factor in Sir Francis's decision. The great house was finished and, to fulfil its full social potential, needed a mistress.

Lady Willoughby insisted on her need for regular medical supervision. In 1589 she was in London 'for the recovery of her health' when she wrote to her husband, saying that 'she has found but little benefit by her medicines, tho' her physicians spare neither his purse nor their own pains, tho' ...... they take but twenty shillings a day and come twice for it.' Despite these considerable charges, she boasted that the cost of housekeeping at Wollaton had fallen since her return the previous year, due to her good management. The outward display of family harmony concealed, not always very successfully, as much back-biting as ever. To keep the potential beneficiaries on their toes, Sir Francis would not settle the future of the estate and, notwithstanding her delicate constitution, Lady Willoughby entered into the game of playing one off against the other with gusto. She was clearly a force to be reckoned with when her temper was up. After one of her many quarrels with Percival, one Alderman Catcher of London wrote to her on Percival's behalf. She gave him short shrift, replying: 'I will forbear to repeat his [ie. Percival's] unfriendly behaviour, because I will not disclose his faults to a babbling fool' and, to drive the message home, signed herself 'a despiser of vain fools, Elizabeth Willoughby.'

Elizabeth's relationship with her eldest son-in-law blew hot and cold. At times she upcast the lean time during her separation, when 'he never sent her any thing, nor lent her a groat'. At other times she promised 'her utmost endeavour to get Sir Francis's estate made secure to him, provided he would help to discharge his debts'. Cassandra commented that 'there are several letters from Lady Willoughby to Percival, some very kind, and others the reverse of them.' A letter to Percival from his brother Edward makes it clear that they saw Robert Spencer, Margaret's husband, as a threat. As long as Willoughby's will remained unsettled, the Spencers stood to benefit and Robert expressed the opinion that 'Sir Francis Willoughby was a most wise man for not disposing of his land in his own lifetime, and for his part if Sir Francis should die, he would keep possession of one of the turrets of the new house.' He stirred matters by asserting it was Percival who had kept Bridget from visiting Lady Willoughby when she was separated and, when she expressed disbelief at this because Percival had always said Bridget could visit her whenever she pleased, Spencer replied: 'Sir Percival could afford her little if he could not afford her fair words.'

In 1588 Bridget gave birth to a healthy son named Francis. Percival was in London with Sir Francis and Lady Willoughby, keeping an eye on his interests and, in truth, being kept hanging on. He wrote that 'if Sir Francis had not promised him as he was a Christian to see him satisfied, he [Percival] should not have stayed from her [Bridget] with such grief and vexation of mind as he had now done.' He added that 'Sir Francis seemed to be very glad, tho' as yet he would doe nothing for the child, and was every day in a thousand minds what to do with the estate.' He also conveyed the effect which the glad tidings had upon the devoted grandmother: 'upon the news her mother was sadly out of humour, and vented her anger upon her maids.'

Although she was capable of showing concern for her married daughters' welfare, occasionally fussing about their accommodation and promising them treats when they were pregnant, Lady Willoughby never seems to have formed a close relationship with any of her offspring. When she became very sick, it was Percival who prompted Bridget to send her some delicacies: 'preserved barberries and some cherries, and to send his dog, because they wanted to kill partridges for Lady Willoughby.' He also enclosed 'the copy of a very affectionate letter, which he desired she would write to her mother.' There is no doubt that Percival was hedging his bets by staying in Lady Willoughby's good books, but he clearly thought his wife incapable of herself composing a kindly letter to her own mother.

This distance between mother and daughter is also seen in Lady Willoughby's relationship with the younger girls, none of whom was allowed to marry during their mother's lifetime. The fourth daughter, Winifred, fell in love with Percival's brother Edward and the sentiment was returned, but when a marriage was proposed Lady Willoughby 'flew into violent passions ..... and would by no means be prevailed upon to hear of such a match'. She kept Winifred locked up and would allow no correspondence between the lovers. The couple eventually eloped after her death, but were always short of money and 'were often reduced to very low circumstances'. Her fifth daughter, Abigail, greeted her mother's death as a 'happy deliverance from all their troubles'. Only after losing both her parents did she marry a gentleman from Northamptonshire called William Pargiter. The youngest daughter, Frances, caused animosity amongst the sisters by striving to be her mother's favourite, though it seems to have done her no good. Cassandra records that 'this course did not long keep her mother from using her with as much severity as the rest of her daughters, as appears by her letters, which are full of sad complaints of the hardships which her mother made her suffer.' Having alienated her sisters, Frances eventually ran away with one John Drake. She wrote to her father, pleading that 'her mother's cruelty had forced her to take this course' and stating that, although she knew she was in the wrong, 'only her mother's wrongs could render her excusable'. She asserted that 'Mr. Drake treated her with great respect and took care to preserve her reputation', but she eventually married another, Montague Wood. Cassandra records Frances's letters to her sisters which 'give an account of his barbarity to her, viz., that he had her turned out of doors, beat her, and made her want all the necessaries for life .... so that upon the whole, one may judge that she had a very miserable life.' On the other hand, a letter from Montague Wood to Frances's sister Abigail, dated May 1600, gives his side of the story. In it he complains of Frances's bad behaviour: 'who hathe acquainted herself with a coople of gentlemen, both strangers to her before now and to me, bothe unmarried men and of notorious fame, and hathe yelded soe mutch to her pleasures as she hathe not refused to goo to taverns to sitt with them.'

During Lady Willoughby's final illness, her son-in-law Robert Spencer took the opportunity of broaching the subject of the younger girls' single status, apparently to no avail. It seems that very good matches had been lost because Elizabeth had steadfastly opposed their marrying, 'upon which account the world blamed her'. He asserted that it was considered 'very unnatural in her, and she must expect God would lay the burden of their offences upon her if they should do otherwise than well.' He warned that: 'should God call her, she might be sure that Sir Francis would marry again, and that she might judge what regard would be had of her children.' His words were prophetic.

Chapter 5: 'The Whore'

In the Spring of 1595, Lady Willoughby's health was giving sufficient cause for concern for Sir Francis to make a complete overview of his affairs. In April he summoned Percival to meet him in London, and to bring with him the rents of three Warwickshire manors and the accounts of the ironworks. More significantly, he was to bring the legal papers which secured his and Bridget's inheritance of Wollaton, Sutton Passeys, Cossall, Trowell, Middleton and Kingsbury. The couple had settled in the house at Middleton by this date. Sir Francis proposed that Percival should reassure the six manors to Sir Francis and his heirs and in return was to receive a dowry equal to that which Margaret's husband, Robert Spencer, had been given. He was also to be discharged of all bonds and covenants with which he was bound with his father-in-law. Percival was being reduced to the same status as the husbands of the younger girls, and it looked suspiciously as if Sir Francis was planning another family. Percival demurred, but two months later Lady Willoughby died. The immediate impact of her death was that the entire household began to accuse one another of stealing her clothes and jewels. More ominously, now that Sir Francis was a free man, their minds were concentrated on the future of the estate. Abigail seems to have been naively alone in her 'hopes for happier days', expecting to take her mother's place as mistress of Wollaton.

Having failed to get Percival's co-operation in April, Sir Francis summoned him again in July, this time to Wollaton. We do not know the detail of what passed between them, but there was clearly a row and Percival left next day without taking leave of Sir Francis, writing to a friend shortly after that his father-in-law was bent on his 'utter undoing'. The day of Percival's departure, July 23rd, also saw the despatch to London of Sir Francis's steward, Russell, 'to seek him a wife'. It was alleged that at Sir Francis's first meeting with the lady, her step-father came with a deed of engagement already drawn up, which Willoughby signed within two hours. The couple were married in August. The speed with which the whole affair was supposed to have been concluded seems so preposterous that it must be suspected the bride had already been selected and the affair kept secret until the interview with Percival on July 22nd, which the younger man found so distressing. Willoughby's new wife was Dorothy Tamworth, a widow, although she had allegedly been separated from her first husband. Cassandra describes her as 'a woman of a great deal of wit', who 'had been called in question for her honesty'. She saw the hand of Sir Francis's servants in bringing about the match, although there is no evidence to support this conclusion other than blame was laid at their door by the family at the time. Cassandra frequently sought to excuse the behaviour of her forebear, readily laying blame on his household: 'some of these gentlemen servants which Sir Francis retained had ..... gained his friendship so much as to have thereby a power to persuade and influence him in the affairs of his family, and this power (I believe from the old papers) they used only for their own advantage'. If they had engineered the match, however, Cassandra reports that they found Dorothy to be made of stronger stuff than either the first Lady Willoughby or Percival and in no wise ready to be used as a puppet: 'This second lady defeated their projects and soon shewed she had subtlety enough to outwit them, so much as to make all their plotting turn to her own advantage, and thereby to gain to herself such immense wealth .... by making use of the declining age and last part of Sir Francis Willoughby's life.' Willoughby was forty-nine years old. She was twenty years his junior and 'took great care to please and oblige him, and thereby soon gained absolute power over him.'

The marriage had been contracted in such a hurry that no firm settlement had been made in writing. Initially, he planned to settle a jointure of 2,000 marks a year on her, secured by various manors, but she preferred to have the land and, since the matter was still unsettled, began to work on him to bring this about. This was very much to Percival and Bridget's disadvantage but, according to Cassandra, Dorothy and the gentlemen servants 'had worked up Sir Francis to such a degree of anger against Sir Percival and his Lady that he did not care what become of them.' A month after the wedding, Sir Francis gave notice that Bridget and Percival were to quit his house at Middleton. There was even an attempt to evict the couple by force, despite the fact that Bridget was pregnant at the time, but the attackers gave up 'after having broke down a wall and two doors'. Percival took his case to the court of Chancery, hoping to have his rights secured.

Bridget blamed Fisher, one of the gentleman servants, for their plight and wrote him a most acrimonious letter. She accused him of having slandered many ladies, including herself, of turning her father against her husband, and of going back on an earlier promise to oppose her father's second marriage: 'to take that stumbling block out of my way, and yet now no man so ready to cog and dissemble with them as thyself.' She stated that he had borne her nothing but malice since she, as a young girl, had resisted his attempt to marry her to his cousin, the notorious Cludde: 'a poor cozening knave of my father's that came lousy to him, and therefore in thy heart [thou] couldst never since abide me.' This incident must have taken place, if at all, over fifteen years earlier, but illustrates how deep were the old wounds that were being torn open once again. The deterioration in the relationship between Sir Francis and his eldest daughter can be judged, not only by his attempt to turn her out of doors, but by a letter of February 1596 in which he demanded the return of certain items belonging to her mother: 'a velvet gown, and much other apparel containing many pearls, and also a great quantity of bothe fine and courser linnin ..... to send him by the bearer, for he will not suffer her to rob and spoile him'.

In the meantime, Sir Francis had set up home in London. He had taken 'a house with fifteen beds', and his mother-in-law formed part of the *menage*. His stewards were instructed to sell some land, he was leasing more and also cutting down timber. In fact he was making a positive effort to reduce his debts, which exceeded £21,000, and managed to repay £14,000 in just over a year. But the family feared that it was his new wife who was reaping the benefit and that the estate would be left impoverished. In April 1596 Percival wrote that when Willoughby's new lady and her friends 'have plombed [plucked] him bare, he may sit like a bird to be a scorn to all the world'.

'A monstrous stir'

By the autumn of 1596 the realisation of Percival's worst nightmare was confirmed: Lady Willoughby was pregnant. The family had endured one false alarm earlier in the year, when Sir Francis declared triumphantly 'it is but an equal lay whether it be a son or a daughter, and if it prove a son, what a monstrous stir.' If Willoughby looked forward to these ructions with gusto, he did not live to witness the event. After a short and violent illness, he died in London on November 16th 1596. Cassandra wrote 'there is a tradition in the family that his friends suspected his lady had given him poison, but whether that be so or not is uncertain.' His personal servant, William Atkinson, told the family that one evening he had been allowed to go and join in the celebrations to inaugurate the new Lord Mayor, even though he had not sought permission to do so. The same evening, Sir Francis had gone to dine at the Fleet, the infamous debtors' prison, where his mother-in-law's husband, Sir Michael Mullins, was an official. Atkinson reported that his master's illness began the next morning, implying that he had been deliberately got out of the way while Sir Francis was poisoned. Willoughby lay ill for about two weeks, and Percival reported to Bridget that 'her father's case was lamentable .... shut up from his friends, that the whore and her minions had stripped him both of goods and land, and left him with nothing where he lay but what hung on his back, and that in this case he [Percival] was solicited to see him.' A few days before succumbing, Atkinson reported that Sir Francis cried 'away with poison' on being offered a bowl of broth. Sir Francis died in the morning and was buried the same night, none of the family being informed. Bridget was outraged at the lack of ceremony attending her father's interment.

The family now had to wait on tenterhooks for almost six months for the birth of the baby. They were taking no chances. Percival applied to the queen for permission to mount a guard on Dorothy's house and to search everyone who visited. Certain women were to be appointed to make a daily inspection of the mother-to-be, and they should also be present to witness the birth. When Lord Burghley queried these extraordinary measures, Willoughby produced a witness, one John Mitchell of Nottingham, who claimed that Dorothy's stepfather, Mullins, had propositioned his pregnant wife to supply them with an heir if necessary: 'If yours prove a son, and my Lady Willoughby's prove a daughter, that would be a good exchange, you having a son already.' Percival became paranoid about changelings. When a woman gave birth to a son in the house next to Dorothy's, he wrote to Bridget saying 'God knows whether she was not brought there by design.' In the meantime, Lady Willoughby was entitled to keep Sir Francis's entire estate, 'in right of the child she went with', Cassandra commenting that 'this engaged Sir Percival in very expensive law suits.' The tenants of the manors which he stood to inherit if Dorothy's child proved to be a girl were warned by the Council that Percival 'seeketh by some extraordinary means to take advantage of some extreme point in law by your consent or act to defraud both the infant of his inheritance and her Majesty of his wardship .... we can do no less than earnestly convey to require you that you be very wary and forbear to join with the said Percival in any action whereby her Majesty might have cause to convey an hard opinion of you.'

'A wench, a wench'

All London awaited the outcome of Dorothy's lying-in. Percival hovered near Dorothy, resident in his father's house at Lincoln Inn Fields, while Bridget waited for news at Middleton. On May 3rd 1597 Dorothy gave birth to a girl, Frances, and 'for three days all dinners, suppers, [St.] Paul's and Smithfield did only discourse of this news.' The relief of the Willoughby family was palpable and May 3rd was revered in their house as a day of celebration for years to come. When the tidings were conveyed to Percival by the spies he had set to watch over Dorothy's house, their jubilance led to a misunderstanding which was reported to Bridget in a letter from her brother-in-law, John Adams, but which Cassandra chose to omit from her account:

> As soon as it was discovered that this lady was delivered of a female, away comes my cousin Harry Willoughby, Gonalson and Cranwell, and as soon as they came into Lincoln's Inn Fields they flung up their hats and cried "a wench, a wench, a wench", intending to give my brother notice of God's great favour. The whores at the grange, looking out of their windows and seeing the gentlemen, mad as they thought and crying out "a wench, a wench", they thought that the gentlemen of the Inns of Court had been coming to take them and, to garte them, leapt out of their chambers, tumbled down the stairs, happy was she that could fall to the bottom first ....'

It must be said that the image of Dorothy Tamworth as a hard-nosed, gold-digging trollop who preyed on the weaknesses of a foolish old man was constructed entirely from the Willoughby family's rather biased point of view. The language used of her was stark. As she recovered from childbirth, the

Willoughbys revelled in her plight: 'The old whore hath the running of the reins [diarrhoea] with melancholic choler [angry frustration], and looks as if she were .... berayed [dirtied, undone]: the great bellied whore who did hope to lay a cuckoo's bird in a sparrow's nest.' The delicacy of a later age led Cassandra to edit these excessive statements out of her *History*, but her own assessment of Dorothy must have been coloured by them. The charges that the Tamworth faction plotted to substitute a changeling boy have little substance beyond Percival's paranoia: the witness was a Nottingham man who might have been set up by the Willoughbys, while London would have been a more convenient source for a baby boy if the plan had been serious.

The poisoning allegation was based entirely on a rumour put about by one of the Willoughby retainers. Sir Francis's chief symptom was diarrhoea, but the description of his illness is too vague to draw conclusions. No doubt there were many diseases in Tudor London which might have been responsible, although the circumstances of the death, and particularly the rushed nature of the burial, do raise doubts. Percival Willoughby took pains to point the finger of suspicion at his step-mother-in-law, but it must be said that, during the previous year or so, the quarrel between Sir Francis and himself had plumbed depths of bitterness hitherto unknown, and he undoubtedly had more to gain by Sir Francis's death. The accusation that Dorothy poisoned Sir Francis, once she was safely with child, in order to cut and run with her fortune, lacks a certain credulity. Dorothy needed a son to secure her position fully, but there were still many barriers to that goal. Her pregnancy might not have run its full course, and there was only an even chance of her producing a boy if it did. Even if she had produced a son, the rate of infant mortality across all classes was so great at that time that she could not be sure of the child's survival. Her interests would have been better served by living with Sir Francis until they had a healthy heir and at least one spare. On the other hand, all the elements of chance which were ranged against Dorothy worked in favour of the Willoughby faction: Sir Francis's premature death stacked the odds in their favour by denying her a second or third chance.

'The Divell and all'

As Sir Francis left no will, Dorothy and Percival engaged in a series of law suits over the wardship of baby Frances and the division of the estate. Lord Burghley had appointed his own son, Robert Cecil, as the baby's guardian, but Percival now petitioned for the wardship, sending Burghley a gelding to help him make up his mind. The baby died, probably before the wardship was finally decided. Over another matter, Lord Chancellor Bacon was given a bribe of £310 by Lady Willoughby when he was acting in a case between the disputants, and this helped bring about his downfall for 'sleaze'. During his life, Sir Francis had given his second wife all his land in Dorset and some property in Nottinghamshire and she was to enjoy a manor at Lambley during her lifetime, after which it was to go to Sir Francis's daughters. Cassandra reiterated the family belief that Dorothy had already carried off the profits that Sir Francis had made from selling or leasing land and timber before his death, but in fact he must have used these revenues almost entirely in paying off debts. Another family tradition was that Dorothy stripped all the houses of their contents. This was probably an exaggeration, although as late as 1610 Thomas Ridgeway, whose daughter was about to marry Sir Percival's eldest son, was given a grand tour of the Willoughby property and commented on 'the apparent marks of a mother-in-law [ie. step-mother] within doors'. Dorothy's story had a less than happy ending, though. She remarried only seven months after Willoughby's death. Her third husband, Philip Wharton, was a baron who believed she was a good catch, but the cost of her law suits disillusioned him and their marriage broke down after only one year. She claimed he deprived her of her property and left her penniless.

The courts confirmed Percival's right to the six manors he had been led to expect by his marriage settlement, including Wollaton. In addition, there was some more property in Nottinghamshire and Warwickshire, some manors which were mortgaged to Lady Arabella Stuart, Bess of Hardwick's grand-daughter, and the ironworks, which were encumbered by debt. The cruellest cut was that Percival was made responsible for Sir Francis's undischarged borrowings of £7,000, while Lady Willoughby escaped any liability for this debt. Bridget's three youngest sisters were to be provided with a marriage portion of 2,000 marks each from his estate and they quickly filed a suit against him to recover this money. Not content with this, the Willoughby girls claimed that the manors excluded from Bridget's marriage settlement, notwithstanding they were mostly mortgaged to Arabella Stuart, should be shared amongst all the Willoughby daughters, including baby Frances. Bridget's nephew, John Spencer, joined their petitions to claim his mother Margaret's share, since she had died. At the same time, Percival was being legally assaulted from his own family, notably his step-mother. Percival's father had died a few months before Sir Francis, leaving the bulk of his estate to him. One manor was to be divided amongst the other sons of Sir Thomas's first marriage and some property was left to his second wife and her children. The remainder of his lands were to go to pay his debts, but any residual capital from this transaction was to go to the second family. This claim was now pressed, Percival's step-mother 'making horrid and unjust complaints of them [ie. the first family] to her children.' Percival resisted, insisting that, far from producing a surplus, the sale had left him with a shortfall of £2,000. As one court case arising from his inheritance was settled, another was fostered, so that by 1598 Percival was engaged in twenty-three legal actions, a web which continued to entangle him for decades.

Bearing in mind the complications brought about by second marriages, then the product of shorter life spans and the hazards of childbirth, it is perhaps understandable that the tradition of the wicked step-mother had become deeply entrenched in popular mythology. We have already seen the reputation which was built up around Dorothy Tamworth. Cassandra, who herself suffered at the hands of a rapacious step-father, blamed Percival's step-mother for depriving his brother Edward of money after he eloped with Winifred Willoughby: 'to raise as much as she could for her own children, [she] might prevent his [ie. Sir Thomas Willoughby] being very kind to his son Edward.' Contemporary attitudes towards the afflictions caused by step-mothers is summed up in a letter of December 1596 to Percival from a friend: 'He writ that whoever encountered with one mother-in-law [ie. step-mother] had enough to doe; but he that had to deal with two had the Divell and all; from whom he prayed God to send him a good deliverance.'

Chapter 6: 'In very plentifull manner': Percival and Bridget's occupation of the hall

A decade after the completion of the great house, Wollaton Hall had barely been occupied. Sir Francis had remained in residence at the Old Hall, using the new building only for special occasions, and had spent the short span of his second marriage mostly in London. A family had been installed in the hall to act as caretakers and the cost of running the place in 1598, without the owners actually living in it but including 'husbandry, repairs, workmen, weeders, etc.', was £588. This exceeded by £3 the entire revenue of the manor for the same year. The silhouette of the house, louring on the horizon over Wollaton village, must have acted as constant reminder of the role the building had played in the current misfortunes of the family and the tongues of the practical people of Nottinghamshire were wagging once again. In 1596 the rector of Wollaton wrote to Bridget at Middleton, begging her to consider taking up residence at the New Hall. No doubt he had an eye on the economic benefits that would accrue locally if the family lived at the big house, but he was also concerned that the Willoughby name was attracting mockery. He wrote 'that in regard it had been lately built by her father at a great expense and was now called Willoughby's Glory, [it] would, if not dwelt in, soon be termed Willoughby's folly ....'. Cassandra summed up Percival's difficulties admirably: 'to have Wollaton house without an estate sufficient to support the grandeur of it in those days was a great aggravation of his misfortunes and made him choose to live more at some of his other houses than there till he could bring his affairs into better posture than Sir Francis had left them.'

Despite their financial difficulties, however, Bridget and Percival managed to keep house 'in very plentifull manner'. Between Christmas Eve and January 8th 1597, at a time when they were wracked with worry over the forthcoming birth of Bridget's half-sibling, they spent £103 1s 3d on Christmas and New Year festivities at Middleton. In 16 days the household got through 7 carcasses of beef, 22 sheep, 2 pigs, 1 goat and 5 1/2 calves. The game comprised 136 rabbits, 6 does, 18 woodcocks, 46 snipe and a couple of partridges, and there were also copious amounts of fish and poultry, including 39 geese. The puddings required 90lb of dried fruit and £6 was spent on claret and sack. The household would have brewed its own beer, for which £16 2s 0d was spent on malt, enough to make 27 hogsheads.

When, in August 1599, Bridget and Percival decided to follow the advice of the vicar of Wollaton and move into the great house, they entertained local society lavishly. It is unlikely that they did much to the house, although another of Thomas Ridgeway's comments suggests that Sir Francis had left the grounds unfinished and that Percival and Bridget had much to do in the gardens. Now they were in residence, the cost of running the house rose to £816 7s 9d, but the yearly average income from Wollaton manor at the time was under £560. To make ends meet, as well as maintaining his numerous law suits, Percival was robbing Peter to pay Paul. The sums he dealt in were small compared with his father-in-law's borrowings, but the transactions were numerous and regular. As some mortgages and debts were cleared, others were taken on in a constant financial juggling act, but sometimes it was difficult to keep all the plates spinning in the air at once. In November 1601, when his credit hit a bad patch, Percival pawned plate for three months for £70 and Bess of Hardwick's son, William Cavendish, lent him £100 the same month: Christmas was coming. Two months later his uncle Henry advised Percival to sell land and clear the debts, reminding him that his father-in-law had started by borrowing £500 and ended by owing £20,000. Interest rates were still pitched at 10%.

A royal visit

In 1603 Wollaton Hall was finally graced with a royal visit, the coveted goal and ultimate object of its former owner's ambition. At last the facilities Sir Francis had been careful to supply would be fully utilized, although it meant that the household finances were further stretched. It is ironic that the honour fell to Percival, with whom Sir Francis had quarrelled so bitterly, and Sir Francis's ghost might have been equally rattled that Percival received his knighthood the same year, surely no coincidence. Queen Anne of Denmark, James I's wife, and her eldest son, Prince Henry, stayed the night of June 21st. They were travelling *en route* from Scotland to London to join the king, who had set off in April a few days after hearing of Queen Elizabeth's death. The royal pair would have reached the capital in good time for the coronation, which took place on July 25th. It was undoubtedly the fame of their building which led to the Willoughbys being singled out for the honour of this visit: only five years later the Duke of Wurtemburg also included the house in his itinerary of the architectural highlights of England and Scotland.

The royal party's short stay occasioned some flurry in the Willoughby household. Masons, carpenters and labourers were hastily summoned to carry out repairs, costing £15 5s 3d, while 12s 4d was spent on painters to spruce up the interior. They concentrated their efforts on fitting new bed-knobs for hangings, which they decorated with gold and silver leaf, but they also painted and

Ill. 38. A bust of Charles I was added to the south facade of the house several years after his visit, as Duke of York, in 1604

gilded baked meats. Yards of cloth and ribbon were brought in, as well as wire and 100 pins, to hang the beds and to dress the dining tables, and someone was paid 2d for carrying in flowers. An extra six dozen spoons and three dozen glasses had to be bought, while 4d was paid for swans' quills to embellish some of the dishes. 4lb of soap was got in ready for the clearing up operation. The menu included 'eight greene fishes, six capons, one dosen chickins, fowre pigs' bought in Nottingham, with perhaps some game from the park. The bill for provisions bought at Nottingham amounted to £70 8s 9d, to cover one night's stay. The visit must have been a success, for it was followed in 1604 by one from the young Duke of York, who eventually succeeded to the throne as Charles I.

Ill. 38

'A lady fit for business'

None of the discord which characterized her parents' marriage is apparent in Bridget's. Cassandra noted that Bridget's letters revealed 'a great deal of spirit' and summed her up as 'a lady fit for business.' Like her mother, she never failed to speak her mind, but through all their vicissitudes, over the inheritance, their financial troubles or worries about their children, she and her husband generally managed to pull together. Her early family life perhaps had the effect of equipping her to face adversity with fortitude for, despite a household which occasionally descended into near chaos, she was always able to cope. On 30th January 1594 she wrote to Percival to inform him of the safe delivery of a child:

> it had pleased God to send them a fourth boy, but all things fell out so cross at the time of her labour that she kept her little wit with much adoe, having hardly a servant at home, and instead of usefull people [a] store of children and dogs, and [she was] forced to take up with a goodwife [ie. housewife from the village] instead of her midwife, which was but cold comfort to her, and should be a warning to her hereafter to be better provided.

Percival was not spared the sharp end of Bridget's tongue when she judged the situation merited it. With a house full of company and Percival away from home, she wrote to him : '[having] no small resort of company to the house, which occasioned great charges ..... 'tho he had left her with those that could do all things well, yet she presumed they could not make money .....' She added, however, that 'she desired he would content himself, and if she be angry, let that away as it came,' and this seems to have been the secret of the relationship's success. Her bark was worse than her bite and Percival was able to 'pass it by', unlike his prickly father-in-law, who could brook no criticism, especially from a woman. However, it must be remembered that Bridget's situation was happier than that of her mother, who had brought no fortune, not even the promised dowry. Bridget was theoretically a great heiress, even if the inheritance was terribly encumbered.

'Perpetually dunned for money'

Sir Percival seems to have managed his county role as well as he could. After becoming Knight of the Shire in 1603, he was elected to Parliament in 1604, but his life was dogged by financial embarrassment, which led to a spell in the Fleet prison in 1606. His regard for his wife was such that he did his utmost to shoulder the burden of their dire financial straits without impinging on her inheritance. This might explain why he did not take his uncle's advice earlier and sell off land. In the event, he sold his own land first before 'he gave his lady the trouble of parting with any considerable lordship which had been her father's.' He also followed his father-in-law in trying to solve his problems by enterprise and enjoyed about as much success. Lack of capital probably frustrated the prosperity of the ironworks, which eventually fell by the wayside, but there were other ventures. The Wollaton coalmine had been overworked and had suffered drainage problems for some time, so that it was no longer very profitable. In 1602 Sir Percival went into partnership with Huntingdon Beaumont, an engineer and entrepreneur who had a plan to revive the industry locally. They leased the pit at neighbouring Strelley, intending to close the Wollaton mine, monopolize the local market from the healthier Strelley pit and also break into the lucrative London market. Robert Smythson, who continued to act as bailiff for the family till his death in 1614, acted as an agent in some of these dealings and it is likely that Beaumont was godfather to Smythson's grandson, who was christened Huntingdon. Despite Beaumont's imaginative approach to the industry, installing at the pit in 1605 the first wooden railway in Britain, the plan failed. Sir Percival bailed out in the nick of time, but pursued his erstwhile partner for the recovery of some of the capital until Beaumont died in prison almost twenty years later.

In 1612 Sir Percival responded to the prospectus of an inventor, Simon Sturtevant, who was selling shares in a company which aimed to profit from his 'mechanical arts and inventions'. Not surprisingly, the company failed and the investment was entirely lost. Four years later, in an equally hopeless venture, Sir Percival's gaze was directed towards the New World, from whence flowed glowing reports of untold wealth from untapped resources. To be fair, from the restricted viewpoint of the Old World, it must have been difficult to comprehend the scale of the American continent and the geographical and climatic variations it encompassed. Sir Percival's investment was to be in a company setting up farms in Newfoundland, for which he borrowed the capital. A party set out in April, the Willoughby's third son Thomas being numbered amongst the settlers. A Beeston man named Bartholomew Pearson reported back to Sir Percival after the first winter, when the livestock had been decimated by frostbite. The settlers' problems had started during the outward voyage, the seed corn having been eaten by the ship's rats, and things had gone from bad to worse as the full horrors of the local climate had been revealed to them. Sir Percival was unable to sell his interest, even for ten pence, and graciously gave it to his son Edward.

Sir Percival's last industrial enterprise was setting up a glassworks at Wollaton. A coal carrier called Fossbrooke first put the idea into Sir Percival's mind, for in 1615 an edict banning the burning of wood to make glass was passed, and Fossbrooke suggested that the coal from Strelley, which was not selling well enough, could be put to use in this way, bringing 'wished profittes to your contentment'. John Smythson drew up the design of the works, and permission had to be sought from Sir Robert Mansell, who owned the patent for the glass-making process. However, local demand for the glass proved to be insufficient to justify the outlay, while attempts to build up markets further afield, especially London, were dogged by transport difficulties.

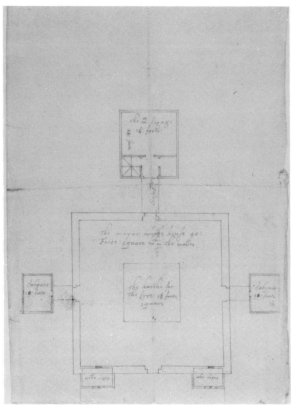

Ill. 39. A design by John Smythson for a glassworks to be built at Wollaton, dated 1615. By courtesy of Hon. Michael Willoughby and the University of Nottingham Library (Mi 165/130).

By the time Sir Percival came to follow the advice given to him twenty years earlier to sell land, economic depression had not only reduced the value of the land, but resulted in a dearth of potential purchasers. His efforts to sell Cossall and Trowell were frustrated and in 1621 the manor of Middleton was seized for debt. There was a tradition in the family that Lady Willoughby had always wished to leave the manor of Kingsbury to her favourite son, Edward, and Cassandra records that Bridget, foreseeing the inevitable break-up of the estate, took steps to secure it for him. She was able to stash away enough capital to buy the manor under a pseudonym, without her husband's knowledge. Perhaps she had, after all, kept more of her mother's pearls than she had been willing to admit.

'This fransie company'

Like all parents with growing children, Percival and Bridget did not escape parental worry. The two eldest sons, Francis and Edward, were sent to Oxford, but were not trained in any profession: the estate was to provide for them and they were brought up as country gentlemen. Francis got the bulk of the surviving estate and married Cassandra Ridgeway, whose father was Lord Treasurer of Ireland, in 1610. Edward got the manors of Kingsbury and Cossall and improved his lot by marrying Elizabeth Atkinson, the heiress of a successful Nottingham physician. The four youngest sons were to make their own way in the world. The third son, Thomas, 'committed some great fault, which made them [his parents] very angry with him', and Cassandra thought that he had run away to sea. It was probably as a punishment, and to keep him out of mischief, that he was sent to Newfoundland in 1616. No doubt the winter of 1617 went some way towards curbing his wanderlust, and possibly contributed to his early death.

The fourth and fifth sons, Henry and Percival, were sent to Oxford at a time when their father 'was grievously oppressed with the want of money'. In 1619 Percival volunteered to alleviate this oppression by giving up his studies. Instead, he was apprenticed to a surgeon, James Van Otten, who undertook to teach him 'musick, physic and surgery, and had promised to use him like a son, maintain him like a gentleman, and to teach him the secrets of physick'. The move proved to be good one, for Percival qualified and had a very prosperous career as a doctor. He wrote a book on midwifery which was reprinted as late as 1863. Henry studied Law and, while still a student, he entreated his father to sell Wollaton 'to clear all at once, for should he but top off some of the principal heads of his debts now, from those roots which remained there would ever spring and bud forth new calamities.' This was sound advice, but as he grew older Henry found it impossible to practice what he preached. Although he was called to the bar in 1620 and eventually to the bench in 1641, his correspondence largely consists of begging letters to various members of the family. In 1627 he wrote flatly that unless his father sent him £200 he would go to prison. Three years later his situation was no better and work clearly disagreed with him. He wrote that 'he would rather dig a grave to bury himself in, than live to be daily engaged, and to be so harassed and tossed in the world'.

Cassandra described the youngest son, Robert, as 'not so industrious as his brothers.' In 1630, starved of cash by his father, he 'took an extraordinary course to help himself, for .... he stole from his father a great many jewels, some plate, a gold cup and spoon, and a great deal of old gold and several odd outlandish pieces.' Six months later he was in prison, though it is unclear whether his father had put him there. It is more likely he was imprisoned for debt, as he begged his father to intercede for him, claiming that he could restore the stolen property and, if only his parents would clear his debts, he 'would be as dutyfull as ever any child was'. The theft had hit Sir Percival very hard: he wrote at the time that 'he had suffered many grievous afflictions, yet this wicked act of his son's was the greatest trouble that he had ever had.'

Four of the Willoughby girls lived to maturity. The second daughter,

Bridget, was the first to marry. In 1606 she married Nicholas Strelley, the son of one of Sir Percival's neighbours, but the lad died young. In 1609 she was back at home, for a household inventory of that year refers to 'Mrs Sturle's Chamber'. It was either the room previously called the Chapel Chamber or one of the painted chambers. The eldest daughter, Theodosia, married Rowland Mynors of Herefordshire in about 1610, a man who shared the afflictions of his in-laws. In 1615 Lady Willoughby wrote to her husband that 'now Nottinggham begines to talke one him [ie. Mynors], and it were not a mise [amiss] they ...... would now doe so mutch as to com paye the mony he hase borrowed in divers places.' In 1621 he wrote to his father-in-law explaining why he had just spent a year in prison for debt, but 'now he assured Sir Percival that he would be a new man and endeavour to retrieve his past errours'. He asserted that he was not fishing for an increased marriage portion, considering that 'in such a wife he had wealth enough.' The third daughter, Elizabeth, was married in 1609 to John Gell of Derbyshire, a match which seems to have aroused little comment in the family archive.

By February 1615 Bridget's behaviour was causing her mother concern. She had formed a liaison with Henry Cavendish, the natural son of Bess of Hardwick's eldest son, Henry. The Willoughbys did not approve, and the antics of the pair had become a source of local gossip. Lady Willoughby's practical nature had resigned her to make the best of bad job, however, and she encouraged her husband to comply: 'Your goodwill must be asked in this bisines; but whether you like it ore noe, it must goe forwards and be a matche'. She advised Sir Percival 'it were not amise if you coulde spare some dayes to com downe [from London] and safe all our credites, which she hath lost'. She described a recent incident when the suitor's coach horses had broken free as he waited for his mistress to finish her toilette:

> for her [he] is everie day sending to her, and she going thether, and t[w]o days agoe he cam hether for her with my Ladies carrouche [coach] and four footemen to attend her, besides horsemen. But my Ladies horses toke a flinging while the[y] stayd for your dater's triming, and brocke my Ladies caroche, overthrew the man, and t[w]o of the horses rane to Nottinggam, and t[w]o the[y] catched in the connyber [rabbit-warren] with mutche adoe. Yet this visious gentle-woman with like maide went forward afote, and ther staid tell darke night ....

After some comments on a minor dispute with Theodosia, Lady Willoughby signs her letter: 'And thus hoping onse to be freede of this fransie company and to be at some beter quyet, I rest, Yours, B.W.' Three days later she was in a panic that the marriage between Bridget and Cavendish would go ahead, not only without their blessing, but without any contract which might safeguard their daughter's future security: 'For here is grete forwardnes, and you had neede make som haste downe, to know what shall be assured, otherwise they will be maried, and after assurances will com but slow.' She adds that she would bring her reluctant daughter to London, but fears that 'I am sure he will com up with her, and the riding, flawning, roysting, and flortting by the way will be sutche as every ostelor will talke of it.' The marriage went ahead but, as predicted, Cavendish went to the bad. Eight years later Lady Willoughby was having to assure Bridget of their continuing support, but could not resist reminding her that: 'now too late she found that in displeasing them she had undone herself.' In 1629 Sir Percival petitioned for the wardship of his grandson by this alliance, enlisting the help of Viscount Chaworth of Wiverton. The latter pledged his support, but: 'writ that all his fear was that the debauched man [ie. Cavendish] would not doe him the favour to dye, who was yet swearing and bowling [boozing] in the Fleet ....'

The youngest Willoughby girl, Lettice, was taken under the wing of her namesake, the ageing Countess of Leicester, Robert Dudley's widow. This lady clearly considered that the Willoughbys were incapable of bestowing their daughters sensibly, for she entreated Sir Percival: 'since he had dealt so liberally with the rest of his daughters, not to let sink the happyness of this .... and this daughter would yeald him more comfort than all his other daughters.' Cassandra transcribed a letter young Lettice wrote to her brother Henry, who was then practising Law at the Inner Temple, asking him to arrange the mugging of one of her ex-suitors with whom she had fallen out:

> This filthy knave is now at London ...... I assure myself you will not let him come so near you and escape scott free. Yet I would not have you fowle your own fingers with so dishonourable a man as he is. I know that about London there are enough that for a price of money will pet a hundred such cowards as he is, and whatever it cost I will pay you again. I would have it to be some one, that he should never find out after ..... but let them tell him they are kinsmen of mine, and that they doe it for the wrong which he had done me, and that it if he does not make sattisfaction he shall not escape so. Thus by your means I hope to hear this worshipfull gentleman will be fain to tarry behind his brother, because he will be so lamed that he had best take a little counsil of the surgion.

The Countess's numerous efforts to fix up the gentle Lettice with a favourable match came to nothing, doubtless due to her father's difficulties in settling a decent sum on her. In 1630 she married a widowed doctor of Divinity who died four years later, asking to be buried beside his first wife.

Chapter 7: Death and Resurrection

Lady Willoughby died in July 1629 and in 1633 Sir Percival, in his eightieth year, described his own physical condition, 'the decays of his weather beaten cottage and carkas', to his brother Robert: 'his hands tremble, his legs totter, his hearing fails, his eyes grow dim so that he can make but little use of his books which are his best friends. His head ..... was grown heavie and dull, and his memory very weak, and all the faculties of his body were decaying.' Sir Percival struggled on in this pitiable state for another ten years. The family had all left home and he rattled around the massive hall with a few servants to look after him.

In 1642 Sir Percival already had a monument to himself and his wife prepared and ready to be installed in Wollaton church. Lacking only the date of his death, it lay waiting in the Gallery but, in the event, a copy had to be made. The memorial was broken up by the heat of a fire which damaged the hall in the same year. From Cassandra's description we can deduce that the south and east wings were most affected. The worst damage seems to have occurred in the area of the north-east corner chamber, traditionally the master's bedroom, which might confirm the family tradition that Sir Percival himself, in his frail state, had caused the fire. The insertion of a massive tie beam half way up the wall between the master's bedroom and the inner chamber to its south may well be the most tangible sign of emergency repairs, which we know cost only £311 14s 8d. Many of the interiors were devastated, the furnishings, decorative paintwork and plasterwork, timber panelling and sculptured fireplaces being destroyed. But the damage, though it caused great loss, was superficial rather than structural. Sir Percival spent the remaining year of his life confined to those rooms which had escaped the conflagration and when he died, in August 1643, the doors remained closed on the ravaged apartments: no one had bothered to clear the wreckage.

For forty-four years the great house lay empty. Its sullen peace was disturbed only once, when a small garrison was billeted in it for a short time during the Civil War. Sir Percival's heir, Sir Francis, was fifty-five when his father died and had been comfortably settled at Middleton since 1615. He and Lady Cassandra lived a quiet life, 'perfectly happy in the agreement of their tempers and inclynations', and had no intention of moving to Wollaton. The tattered remnants of the Willoughby legacy had fallen to a couple who abjured the limelight but worked steadfastly towards restoring the family finances to a sound footing. Their grand-daughter Cassandra states clearly that they chose to remain at Middleton 'out of good husbandry' and an unwillingness to undertake the cost of restoring the stricken hall. Their heir, Francis Willoughby F.R.S., devoted most of his life to academic research. His short but very distinguished career allowed no opportunity for a resumption of residence there either.

Ill. 40.
Ill. 41.

Ill. 40. Sir Francis Willoughby II (1588 -1665), whose
economy restored the financial health of the family.
By courtesy of Hon. Michael Willoughby

Ill. 41. Cassandra Ridgeway (1599 -1675), daughter of
the Lord Treasurer of Ireland and wife of Sir Francis
Willoughby II. By courtesy of Hon. Michael Willoughby

Francis the Naturalist

Ill. 42.

Francis was destined to become the most eminent of all the Willoughbys.
He went to Sutton Coldfield school and on to Trinity College, Cambridge,
where he studied the Liberal Arts. His interest, however, lay in the natural world
and he was very much influenced by John Ray, a blacksmith's son who had
risen to become a tutor at the university. Francis became involved in Ray's
botanical researches and a life-long partnership sprang up between them. Ray
remained more interested in plants, while Francis's fascination turned towards
zoology. The pair made journeys of discovery throughout the British Isles and
Europe, some of Francis's best work being inspired by new techniques being
developed at Padua University. Their collaboration resulted in a series of
publications in which they evolved a system of classification which under-
pinned all future study of plants and animals. Willoughby's *Ornithologia and
Historia Piscium* became seminal works, revealing new insights into the animal
kingdom based on his powers of scientific observation. He became a founding
member of the Royal Society in 1662.

Francis was thirty when he inherited the Willoughby estate, but he had
devoted himself too assiduously to study to get married. His brother-in-law,
Sir Thomas Wendy, now began to nag him to turn his attention to securing

the future of the Willoughby line and suggested a copious number of candidates. In the event, Francis chanced upon his own choice and married Emma Barnard in January 1667. The couple lived at Middleton with his mother, Lady Cassandra, and had two sons and a daughter. The girl, named after her grandmother, grew up to be the amateur historian responsible for the preservation of much of the detail of the Willoughby annals. She clearly took after her father but, being female, was not given his education. Although she was only two when he died, too young to have been influenced by his daily routine (a brief walk before lunch and the rest the day devoted to his books), she too was to spend long hours sorting, classifying and transcribing the Willoughby papers, as well as putting her father's notes and specimens into order. She, too, was so absorbed and content in her walk of life that she only married, at the age of forty-three, when she thought it would be more considerate for the family for her to do so than to remain single.

Ill. 42. Francis Willoughby, F.R.S., the famous naturalist (1635-By courtesy of Hon. Michael Willoughby

The Willoughby family were firmly convinced that Francis's devotion to study 'very much impared his health and shortned his life', contributing to his premature death at the age of thirty-seven. Since his foreign travels, he had been prone to recurring attacks of fever, succumbing to the last in July 1672 after having lain ill for a month. He left three children, the eldest only four years old, and, in true family tradition, a law suit. A distant relative, Sir William Willoughby of Selston in Nottinghamshire, had adopted Francis as his heir, having no son of his own, and had left him the manors of South Muskham and South Carlton near Newark, which were worth about £1,200 a year. Sir William had fallen out with his only sister when she married Sir Beaumont Dixey, whom Sir William disliked. The two manors formed a very small part of Sir William's estate, but were the only element he had the power to dispose of as he wished. Nevertheless, Dixey pursued first Francis and later his son vainly through the courts for their recovery. Although the Willoughbys spent around eight thousand pounds defending their right to the property, the investment was worth it in that the land helped swell the depleted Willoughby estate.

'Hardly used by their father-in-law'

In his will, Francis left £60 a year to John Ray, requesting that he should remain with the family at Middleton to tutor his sons. All went well for a few years until the elderly Lady Cassandra died in 1675, and the following year Emma remarried. Francis, the eight-year-old Willoughby heir, took a marked dislike to his stepfather, Sir Josia Child, an astute business man who had made a sizeable fortune as Governor of the East India Company. The trouble might have begun when John Ray refused to move to Wanstead in Essex, the home Child had recently purchased 'at prodigious cost'. The Willoughby boys were now taught by 'a very indifferent tutor', along with their stepbrother, a lad of 'inferior wit', according to Cassandra. Young Francis, bored by his education and companion, clearly resented the fact that Sir Josia refused to send him away to school, for Child believed that children 'born to estates' should not be entrusted either to public schools or universities. Francis's resentment was heightened by the knowledge that the tutor he found so wanting was being paid out of his own inheritance. Young as they were, the three children seem to have been fully aware that their stepfather was exploiting his position as their guardian to the full, drawing expenses for their upbringing which were, in their opinion, out of all proportion to the actual costs involved.

By the age of twelve, Francis was ready to take his own future in hand. Emma's sister had married Lord Chandos, who was about to leave England to take up an ambassadorial post in Constantinople. Francis begged to be taken along, but his uncle advised him that at his age he would do better to stay at Wanstead with his mother. A similar application to another uncle in London produced the same response. Francis, becoming more desperate, ran away from home. On taking his morning ride, he simply kept going until he reached the Cambridgeshire home of his paternal aunt, Lettice Wendy, arriving just before supper on June 3rd 1680. Lady Wendy, now in her early fifties, had lost her husband while still young but had never remarried. Both of her own children had died at birth and Francis found her more welcoming than his uncles. She took him in with open arms, calling him 'her dear jewel'. It was agreed that Francis could stay with his aunt and his clothes were sent on, along with a message of good riddance from his mother, which he never forgave. Emma was caught between her children and her husband. Cassandra confessed that she herself, then aged ten, had caused her mother further aggravation by pestering to be allowed to follow her brother, a wish which was not granted. There are indications in Lettice Wendy's letters that, after the first flush of joy at receiving the precious boy, the realities of bringing up a spirited twelve-year-old lad were beginning to dawn on her consciousness. Although very tempted to send him to school, she eventually settled on a resident tutor and, after two years, Francis went to St Catherine's College, Cambridge, taking his tutor with him. Freed from the sobriety of Aunt Wendy's ordered and highly religious household, the pair seem to have a very good time indeed, considerably overspending Francis's allowance. The blame for this profligacy was firmly laid by Aunt Lettice at the door of the tutor, for 'such liberties as ill became a clergyman', and also on the master and fellows of Catherine Hall, who were 'so very deficient in their care of the young students'.

By 1684, Sir Josia Child 'was weary of the trust' of dealing with his stepsons. He had long given up any hope of permanent acquisition of the Willoughby estate through arranging 'cross matches' with offspring from his earlier marriages. The following year, at the age of seventeen, Francis was ready to take his stepfather head on. First he secretly arranged the removal of his thirteen-year-old brother from Wanstead to Cambridge, a plot which the three siblings conspired at. Cassandra explained that, because of the inferiority of his education at Wanstead, Thomas 'was very deficient in learning to make him fit for the university', so Francis placed him in Jesus College, where one of the fellows, Dr. Man, undertook to bring him on. One cannot help but suspect that Francis's own track record at St. Catherine's also had something to do with the choice of a different college. Child was extremely cross when he found Thomas had been spirited away and there were harsh words. As soon as Francis saw Thomas settled at university, he left to take up lodgings in London so that he could devote his time to the serious business of suing his stepfather. His grievances were that Sir Josia was wasting the proceeds of both Francis's estate and his mother's jointure in order to enrich himself, while giving Francis an inadequate allowance. The case was heard by the infamous 'hanging' Judge Jeffreys, the Lord Chancellor, and while it rumbled on, Francis regained control

Ill. 43. The sons of Francis the Naturalist, Sir Francis Willoughby, Bart. (1668-88) and Sir Thomas Willoughby, Bart., First Lord Middleton (1672 - 1729). Their sister was Cassandra, Duchess of Chandos (1670 -1735) - see illustration 2.

of his property. His doting aunt, Lady Wendy, declared that 'she pittyed so young a creatur's being master of so plentifull an income'.

'Mistress of Wollaton'

Cassandra Willoughby was seventeen when her wish to live with her dear brother was finally granted. In October 1686 Francis, now in command of his own affairs, had reconnoitred his estates in Nottinghamshire and found everything 'in great disorder'. He determined to move into Wollaton Hall and restore his inheritance. When he asked his sister to act as housekeeper, she was overjoyed: 'This proposall I was much delighted with, thinking it would be no small pleasure for me to be Mistress of Wollaton, and to doe whatever I had a mind to, believing that such a government would make me perfectly happy'. In midsummer 1687 Francis sent his coach to bring Cassandra to her new home. One can only imagine the reactions of the teenage couple, he nineteen and she seventeen, as they surveyed the house, scanning the weed-ridden grounds, picking their way through the 'heaps of rubbish' left after the fire of 1642, raising the dust of the forty-four years' sleep. Coming at last upon the fragments of their great-grandparents' shattered memorial, it must have seemed like a metaphor for the house itself: at least they had the optimism of youth to sustain them.

After essential works to restore the fire damage and to revive and enlarge the gardens were put in motion, the couple went to Middleton to assess the state of their father's legacy. They were greatly relieved to find his books in better condition than they expected and removed his whole collection, including his specimens, to Wollaton. Despite the restoration work going on around them and a lack of furniture, much of which had gone in the fire, Francis revived the family tradition for lavish entertainment. Cassandra commented that her brother rejected the growing fashion for oval dining tables because the old-fashioned long boards could be placed end to end to accommodate any number of guests. After almost a year Francis decided to make a grand tour and arranged for Cassandra to stay with friends in Ludford. He never got beyond London, where he hoped to end his wrangles with Sir Josia Child before leaving the country. In July 1668, at the age of twenty, he fell ill and died within two months. Cassandra never saw him again. Sixteen-year-old Thomas had left Cambridge with his tutor, Dr. Man, to be at his brother's bedside, and never returned to his college. Having arranged a funeral at Middleton, he stepped into his brother's shoes, not least in engaging with Child. Thomas was at some disadvantage because of his extreme youth and he also suffered an attack of smallpox which nearly carried him off. Cassandra relates the deleterious effects on her mother, Emma, of the ongoing dispute between the children of her first marriage and her current husband. It was for this reason, Cassandra claimed, that Thomas eventually settled out of court, despite what he and his sister considered to be unfavourable terms. Cassandra estimated they had been cheated of £60,000, although her figures could sometimes be imaginative. At least Thomas was master of his own inheritance, even if he thought it should have been bigger. Perhaps the scare of the smallpox incident had brought it home to the family that Thomas was the last thread upon which the Willoughby line hung: at any rate, it was decided that travelling on a grand tour was too risky, and he settled down to his role as country gentleman at Wollaton.

Life in the late 17th-century house

The *menage* comprised Thomas, Cassandra and Dr. Man, who abandoned Jesus College to carry on tutoring the young landowner. The household rose at five and Thomas and Dr. Man spent three hours closeted in the library, sustained by tea brought by the servants. Cassandra might have used this time to clean and catalogue her father's collection of 'dried birds, fish, insects, shells, seed, minerals and plants', a task the family would not entrust to servants. Between eight and nine the bell rang for prayers, attended by the whole household. By now the household must have been ready to do justice to breakfast, although this was denied to anyone who had missed prayers without good cause. After breakfast, Thomas and Cassandra went amongst the workmen, engaged both within the house and in the gardens, to supervise plans and check progress. If there was any time before dinner at noon, he or Dr. Man read to her while she worked on needlework intended to recover the furniture. This activity was resumed in the afternoon, unless the couple were receiving guests or going out to visit. Occasionally they went hunting. After dinner, they indulged in leisure activities: walking, bowling, fishing or riding in summer, indoor games in winter. Cassandra recounts that dressing up in the old clothes found in the Wardrobe to imitate the family portraits proved to be an amusing pastime, both to them and their guests. She gives a detailed description of a red velvet gown she felt sure was that worn by Elizabeth Willoughby in her portrait, although all the pearls had been picked off. At ten o'clock the household reconvened for prayers, then went to bed in order to be up by five the next morning. Twice a week, the neighbouring poor were fed with bread, broth and leftovers.

The house was partly refurnished with stuff from Middleton, although the Willoughbys had to get a decree in Chancery before Sir Josia would let them remove it. The very practical Cassandra was outraged that, by that time, they had been forced to buy a lot of linen and plate quite unnecessarily. As we have seen, she worked tirelessly to restore the furnishings, but they also bought some new furniture in London. Since their visits to the capital usually involved much business with the lawyers, Cassandra relates that they had little time to spare for leisure. But she does recall a visit to Greenwich, to see Sir John Flamsteed, the first Astronomer Royal, and their fascination with his collection of astronomical instruments. They also saw 'Mr. Charlton's collection of rarities' which, later acquired by Sir Hans Sloane, became the nucleus of the British Museum collection.

Future assured

The bad blood between the Willoughbys and their stepfather did not sour their relationship with their mother, who came to stay in the summer of 1690, bringing one of her stepsons with her. The sudden death of Dr. Man during this visit came as a great shock to Thomas, whose own life was soon threatened for the second time by serious illness. On his recovery, the time was considered ripe to find him a wife. Many families had sought to acquaint their daughters with Cassandra, a socially acceptable method of bringing their girls to her eligible brother's attention. Now Thomas received a much more direct approach from Sir Richard Rothwell of Ewerby and Stapleford, near Newark, who sent his brother as an envoy to propose a match with his daughter and heiress, Elizabeth. At first the Willoughbys thought the proposal too good to be true, since the Rothwell estate adjoined the Willoughbys' manor of Muskham. Moreover, the bride was to have £10,000 on her marriage and £1,000 per annum. Thomas married her on his nineteenth birthday: the fortunes of the family, already restored to good financial health, were assured. Thomas served as MP for Nottinghamshire and was raised to the peerage in 1712. The Barons Middleton continued to prosper at Wollaton for generations.

On Thomas's marriage Wollaton had a new mistress, but one forms the impression that Cassandra's place as 'housekeeper' was never supplanted, and she remained part of the family. Although she travelled the country, staying with family, friends and acquaintances, she spent most of her time at her beloved Wollaton. The disciplines of natural historian and antiquarian were not dissimilar at that date so, having sorted and catalogued her father's collection and papers, perhaps it was a natural progression for her to tackle the family archive. The job must have taken years, but she seems to have been perfectly content in maintaining a routine which clearly suited her well. Cassandra's *History* breaks off suddenly in mid sentence, just as she recalled the shock, on meeting her sister-in-law for the first time, of finding that she bore an overwhelming resemblance to her dead brother, Francis. We do not know what caused her to abandon her work, although in 1726 she began to suffer from bouts of ill health and this might have been the reason. However, it is more likely that marriage took her from her writing. In 1713, Cassandra received a proposal from her first cousin, James Brydges: she was forty-three, he thirty-nine and recently widowed. Her immensely wealthy husband bought Canons, an Elizabethan mansion in Middlesex and began to convert it into a vast Palladian country house. Cassandra's experience of managing builders must have come in useful, although here she had to deal with some of the leading architects of the day. In overseeing the establishment of this household, she was not required to practice the practical economy she had shown over twenty years earlier at Wollaton. The expense Brydges' lavished on his house, library, picture collection and gardens made it a wonder of the age, just as the newly-built Wollaton had once been. Brydges was created Duke of Chandos in 1719.

Chapter 8: Modernization

The 17th-Century House

When Francis Willoughby decided to salvage the long-neglected house, he found that damage caused by the fire of 1642 had been relatively superficial. Although the loss of many splendid interiors was a cause of considerable regret, at least the structure remained sound. Most of the rooms in the east and south wings had suffered, including the Long Gallery, the Dining Parlour and the Painted Chambers. Cassandra describes how the alabaster and stone chimneypieces had crumbled to dust and the wainscotting had gone. But the floors had been covered with lime plaster which had preserved the joists, so the walls remained well tied. Work to restore the panelling and interior decoration seems to have started as soon as Francis and Cassandra moved in in 1687, and continued under the proprietorship of their brother Thomas.

The one structural problem which had to be addressed had nothing to do with the effects of the fire, but with the composition of the High Hall floor, and it might have been a few years before it became apparent. As we saw in chapter 3, the 'Chinese lattice' design used to span the width of the Great Hall ceiling had an inherent weakness. The joints tended to pull apart, giving rise to fears that the central tower walls were pushing outward. The difficulty would have been avoided had the more convential tie-beam been used in the floor structure. Some time before 1697, an attempt to solve this problem was made by adding buttresses on the north and south sides of the tower (shown in illus. 44). Fortunately, solid walls underlie each buttress right down to ground level. The work was very carefully executed but discrepancies in the coursing show clearly that the buttresses were added to the central tower, rather than being tied into it, as they would have been had they been original. The house appears without the buttresses in a drawing by the artist Hollar, published in 1677 in Thoroton's *Antiquities of Nottinghamshire* (frontispiece).

As social conventions change from age to age, so do the expectations which are required from the design of houses. In the late Tudor and Stuart period it was accepted that the wider household ate and even slept in the Great Hall, as they would have done in the Middle Ages. There had been a progression from the medieval period in as much as the family took their meals in private in a separate Dining Parlour and bedrooms were far more numerous: all family members had chambers and so did the higher-ranking servants. By the late 17th century, however, this was not sufficient. While a large staff was needed to run the house, it was not considered necessary to see too much of them. By now it had become the norm for servants to eat in a hall kept quite separate from those 'polite' spaces in the house occupied by the family. Although there still weren't enough bedrooms for everyone, the servants also had to sleep out

Ill. 44. *Wollaton Hall and Grounds from a painting by Jan Siberechts, 1697. The bird's eye view was based on an earlier engraving by Kip after a drawing by Knyff. By courtesy of Hon. Michael Willoughby.*

of sight. The problem was where to put a servants' hall which could supply these needs. At last it was decided that the Ale Cellar in the basement was the only place which offered enough space and it was also conveniently placed with regard to the kitchens. It had other advantages, like a direct doorway to the western courtyard, so that outworkers, such as gardeners, could come in at mealtimes without tramping through the house. There were, however, two obstacles to the cellar's conversion: it had no heating and, if it ceased to be an ale cellar, where would they store the ale?

Ill. 45.　　The first of these problems was solved by installing a fireplace in the west wall of the cellar. As there was no flue, it was necessary to insert one in the thickness of the wall. From the lowest floor level in the entire house right up to the leads, the wall was laboriously cut away and traces of the making good can be seen on the outer wall. When the leads were reached, a normal chimney pot would have spoilt the appearance of the balustrade, so the flue was disguised inside a hollowed-out baluster and the smoke emerged through a niche in a classical tabernacle. The loss of storage for ale was more than adequately supplied by a much larger ale cellar which was built at the north-west corner of the house, flanking the western courtyard (see chapter 9). In order that this rather utilitarian structure did not detract from the appearance of the mansion, however, it was buried underground: only its doorways fronting the service courtyard would have been visible from the exterior when it was finished.

Ill. 45. A chimney for the servants' hall flue emerged on the leads and was disguised in a baluster. The smoke emerged through the right-hand niche in the tabernacle.

Further underground work carried out on the east side of the house extended the existing provision for wine storage, although the chief motive for executing this work was probably to do with water supply (see chapter 9).

Many features of the interior decoration of this period were swept away in a much more radical overhaul of the house which took place in the 19th century, but one or two have survived. The door-way from the north state staircase into the Great Ill. 46. Hall retains an elaborately carved surround, giving some impression of the taste of the era: much of the replaced interior woodwork would have been in this style. Two artists, whose reputations were growing amongst the owners of country houses, were commissioned to paint the ceiling of the south state staircase and the whole landing area Ill. 47. of the north state stairs. Sir James Thornhill probably worked at Wollaton between 1700 and 1707, when his career was still in the making. He went on to work at Chatsworth. His style was perhaps influenced by Louis Laguerre, a Frenchman who probably worked at Wollaton a little before him. The murals on the north stairs landing would have been interrupted by a window overlooking the Great Hall and a doorway to the leads, which were duly blocked. Perhaps to replace the staircase, but more likely to provide a much easier route to the leads than the narrow and twisting Elizabethan spiral stairs, the western staircase was extended 48. upwards in timber: it had previously reached only as far as the first floor.

The grounds

Cassandra's account makes it clear that enhancing the grounds was given considerable priority in the general scheme of restoration. The area of formal garden on the south side of the house was considered too small, so Francis began to reform it and Thomas greatly enlarged his plan. Thomas Willoughby, taking after his father, had developed an interest in botany at Cambridge and had made

Ill. 46. *This elaborate door surround, added during the time of Thomas and Cassandra, gives an impression of the interior decoration in the early 18th century.*

Ill. 47. *Mural paintings depicting the legend of Prometheus decorate the landing of the north state stairs. A doorway to the leads and High Hall was blocked so that the painting should not be interrupted.*

Ill. 48. This timber staircase, built during the late 17th or early 18th century, extended the Tudor western stairs to provide much easier access to the leads.

a collection of 'physicall plants', that is plants with medicinal qualities. He employed a Mr. Pratt to help establish and expand his collection, which Dr. Man used to treat the neighbouring sick as well as the household and family. Mr. Pratt had worked at the Chelsea physick garden, founded in the 1670s. Cassandra believed he had left because the pay wasn't good enough. In May 1680, around the time he came to Wollaton, the Apothecaries Society learnt that four hundred of their twelve hundred specimens had gone missing.

Ill. 44.　　Judging by a painting of 1697 by Jan Siberechts, the reformed gardens were quite well established by that date and none of the Tudor outbuildings had survived the improvements. Other elements of the Elizabethan layout are still discernable, though somewhat changed. The three squares of formal garden south of the house were retained, their centrepiece a pond with fountains. This pond seems likely to have been part of the Tudor garden for, not only does a circular feature appear in its place in Smythson's design for the house and grounds (illustration 9), but a seemingly original drain runs from it to the Tudor sewer east of the house, so that it could be periodically drained out and cleaned. Siberechts' painting shows the rest of this formal area laid to lawns flanked with trees in tubs and with a larger plantation of trees in the westernmost square. Originally, this whole section of the garden would have been set with elaborate parterres and Cassandra tells us that one of these had been planted with miniature box trees to reproduce the plan of the house. The large flat area of the southern garden had most probably been artificially made up when the house was new. A book of extraordinary household payments of 1591 records many payments to one Richard Gamble 'and his fellows' for collecting and carting stone from the ruined Lenton Priory, some of which might have been used to build a substructure to retain and stabilise the soil. The ground had always sloped away to the south and the young Willoughbys extended the garden in this direction at a lower level, with steps to reach it: it is shown in the painting planted with young trees. They added a terrace walk along the southern boundary of the old garden, where there was (and still is) a steep drop between the two gardens. This was faced with a retaining wall whose construction cut off the Elizabethan sewer on the east side of the house (see chapter 9). The dairyhouse of Smythson's plan, had it existed, would have been swept away by these improvements.

The enlarged southern gardens were also extended towards the east and west and a glass-roofed orangery can be seen in the forefront of the picture. The stables and courtyard, which had occupied the eastern side of the house, were swept away and the ground extended to provide room for a 'D'-shaped bowling green, hedged by rows of trees, a ha-ha and the boundary wall. A two-storey banqueting house beside the green must have taken over much of the function previously served by the tower turret chambers. Wollaton village is depicted in the background, along with a rather idealised landscape. Thomas's son,

Ill. 49. An impressive new stable block was added in 1742 by the 2nd baron. Photo by Chris Salisbury.

Ill. 49.   Francis, added a stable block to the north-west of the house in 1742. The park was further landscaped during the 18th century, including the addition of a lake to the west.

'More comfortable modes of domestic life'

Ill. 50.

Despite the changes made to the house by the Willoughby family at the end of the 17th-century and throughout the course of the 18th century, if one could travel back in time to this era, one would still recognize that Wollaton was an Elizabethan house. The alterations were superficial, leaving the essential plan intact. During the first third of the 19th century this was all to change, for the internal plan became Georgian rather than late Tudor in character. Around 1801, the architect Jeffry Wyatt, who later changed his name to Wyatville because he thought it sounded more impressive, was commissioned by Henry, 6th baron Middleton, to modernize Wollaton. He worked on the house intermittently for over thirty years and by the time he had finished, its original owner would have found some difficulty in finding his way around it. By 1809 Wyatville was renowned as a man 'who has manifested much skill in converting the interior of old, ill-arranged mansions to the present and more comfortable modes of domestic life'. His reputation grew, culminating in a commission to modernize Windsor Castle for George IV, which he began in 1824. He was knighted in 1828.

In the 'polite' areas of the house, Wyatville covered the tracks of his alterations with new plasterwork, cornicing and doorframes, but was much less fussy in those regions of the house occupied by servants. Few examples of Smythson's finishing details survive in the polite areas of the house, but where they do they show that the service areas were treated to the same high standard. Wyatville, by contrast, paid no attention to detail 'below stairs', where his alterations were often clumsy and there was little or no attempt to 'make good'. At least this policy had the fortunate effect of leaving much of the Tudor detail intact, along with many clues as to the original layout and structure. These have made a theoretical reconstruction possible.

Wyatville replaced both state staircases with more elegant cantilevered stairs, though the service staircase was left intact. The only alterations   Ill. 51.

Ill. 50. Henry, sixth Lord Middleton.
By courtesy of Hon. Michael Willoughby

made to this were concerned with suppressing noise. In the Elizabethan house, orders shouted inside the kitchens and in the servery area must have carried up the stairs and into the Great Hall. Wyatville blocked the landing window overlooking the servery and placed doors strategically to muffle such sounds. One was placed at the top of the short series of steps leading out of the servery; one at the foot of the service staircase and another half way up. Lastly, the central doorway in the screens passage, which had previously been an open archway so that traffic would be unimpeded, was fitted with doors.

A plan of the ground floor at Wollaton, published in 1809, helps to trace how far Wyatville's improvements had advanced by that date. The state staircases had been replaced and he had gone to work to improve the convoluted and asymmetrical entrance arrangement of the old house. The porter's lodge and wardrobe were completely swept away to open up the entry space, so that a lobby of balanced, classical proportions could be provided. A doorway was cut in the north wall of the Great Hall, so that one entered it immediately from the entrance lobby. The concept of a 'high' and 'low' end of the Hall had been obsolete for years, so there was no bar to an entrance in the middle. Indeed, the whole function of the Great Hall had changed: it was no longer the hub of an extended household, but used as a grand circulation area or as a ballroom. The screens passage was also obsolete and in 1832 Lord Middleton suggested that the central section of the screen might be removed, but fortunately this was not done. Space previously taken by the old entrance passage was used to provide a porter's room (8 on Briton's plan) and an armoury (9). The spiral staircase shown here on the plan was never actually built.

Ill. 52.

Ill. 53.

Ill. 51. The Georgian north state staircase. Photo by Chris Salisbury.

Most of the bedrooms on the ground floor were converted to other uses. A new dining room (7 on Briton's plan) was created in the north-west corner by knocking down a wall and combining the old Tudor pantry with the north-west corner bed-chamber. Access to this dining room, a high status room, was actually by the old pantry door. In the Tudor house, this would have been unthinkable. The integration of classes in the Tudor household was much greater, for the entire household ate and slept in close proximity. In these circumstances, social hierarchy was maintained by strict distinctions underlined by the architecture, so that which entrance one used, or was allowed to use, would have had real significance. Now that the serving classes were kept separate, eating in their own quarters and housed invisibly at night, the need

54.

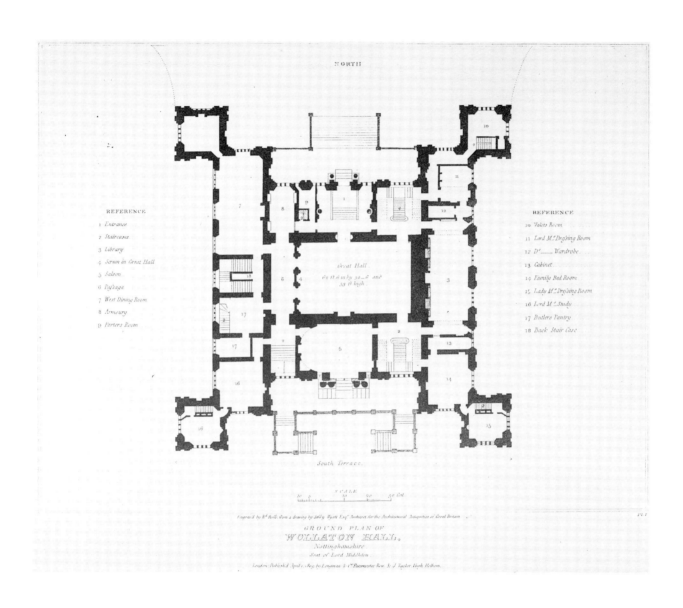

Ill. 52. *This plan of the ground floor, published in J.Britton's 'Architectural Antiquities of Great Britain',*
gives some idea of how far Wyatville's improvements had gone by 1809.

Ill. 53. The re-worked Georgian entrance hall. Photo by Philip Dixon.

for these rules of etiquette was removed and their architectural manifestations disappeared. Lord Middleton would have been unaware that he was entering his dining room by the old pantry door, a portal Sir Francis Willoughby would never have personally approached.

The old 'Garden' or 'Duke's Chamber' in the south-west corner became Lord Middleton's study and the inner chamber beyond became a strongroom (16 on Britton's plan). More radical changes were made to the east wing. The postern door and its staircase were removed, along with the room divisions of the two painted chambers and an inner chamber. These spaces combined to create a spacious library (3 on Britton's plan). The old 'Chapel Chamber' in the south-east corner remained a bedroom (14 on Britton's plan), with a large wardrobe taking up some of the space made available by removing the postern staircase. The inner chamber (15 on Britton's plan) became Lady Middleton's dressing room. The north-east corner chamber (11 on Britton's plan) was considerably reduced in size, being partitioned to allow an access passage from the wine cellar stairs. This left the room, which became Lord Middleton's dressing room, undisturbed by traffic. At this stage the postern door to the garden on the south side was left intact, but the old Dining Parlour had become a sitting room, now called the Regency Saloon (5 on Britton's plan).

Now that there was only one bedroom left on the ground floor, the first floor was made to accommodate many more bedrooms and boudoirs. The two Great

Ill. 55.

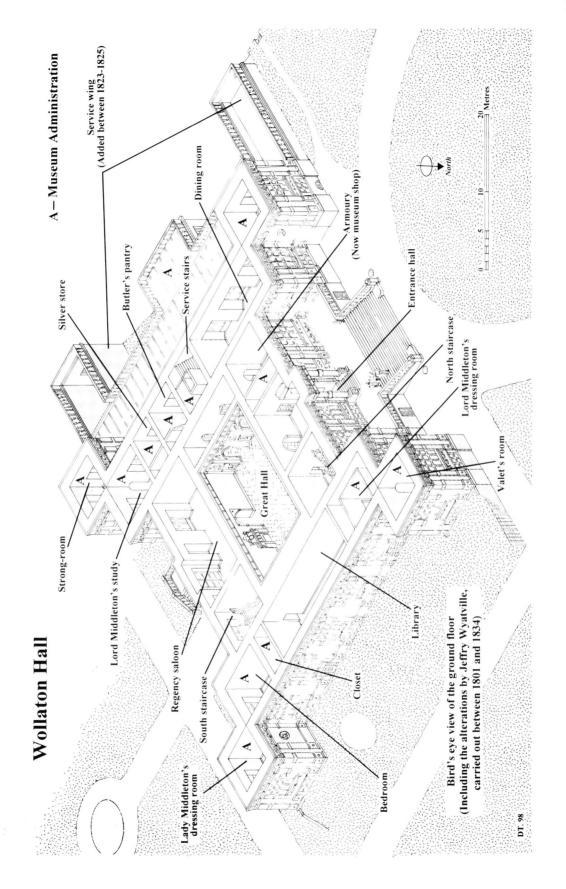

Wollaton Hall

A – Museum Administration

Service wing
(Added between 1823-1825)

Silver store

Butler's pantry

Dining room

Service stairs

Strong-room

Lord Middleton's study

Regency saloon

South staircase

Lady Middleton's
dressing room

Great Hall

Armoury
(Now museum shop)

Entrance hall

North staircase

Lord Middleton's
dressing room

Valet's room

Library

Closet

Bedroom

North

Metres

Bird's eye view of the ground floor
(Including the alterations by Jeffry Wyatville,
carried out between 1801 and 1834)

DT. 98

Ill. 54. A bird's-eye view of the ground floor after alterations during the Georian period. Drawing by David Taylor.

116

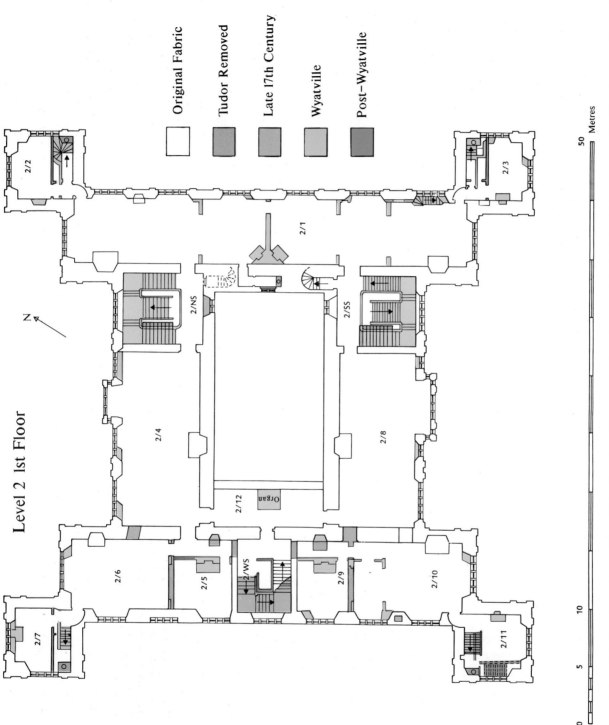

Level 2 1st Floor

Original Fabric

Tudor Removed

Late 17th Century

Wyatville

Post–Wyatville

2/2

2/3

2/1

2/NS

2/SS

2/4

2/8

2/12

Organ

2/6

2/5

2/WS

2/9

2/10

2/7

2/11

0   5   10   50
Metres

Ill. 55. A phased plan of the first floor, showing Wyatville's alterations. The orange colour denotes original fabric which was removed, whilst the green, blue and pink represent newer installations. Drawing by David Taylor.

Chambers must have served as principal bedrooms and were left intact, although much of the fenestration was blocked on the interior. Throughout the house, Wyatville reduced windows to make them look like Georgian sashes, although they were left intact on the exterior to maintain the outward appearance of the elevations. The east and west wings of the first floor were considerably cut up into smaller spaces, the Long Gallery being a particularly sad loss.

Apart from producing bedrooms for family and guests, part of Wyatville's brief was clearly to provide a great deal of unobtrusive sleeping accommodation for living-in servants. The Georgians wished more servants to be housed less visibly, but were indifferent to the quality of their accommodation. The only space left to exploit was between floors. The house already had some chambers at mezzanine level: the cook's chamber in the basement was over the Pastry Kitchen and the inner chambers to the better bedrooms had further small chambers over them. Wyatville multiplied the number of mezzanine level rooms. Virtually all the tower chambers were cut horizontally in two and many had fireplaces added. Extra rooms were placed above the Buttery and Butler's Chamber, and even some of the more polite rooms lost upper space: small mezzanine level suites were placed above Lord Middleton's dressing room and over some of the family bedrooms on the first floor in the east wing

Ill. 56.

(originally the Long Gallery). Some of the new rooms, particularly in the northeast tower, were better finished off than the others, so may have housed family members. Mostly, however, the mezzanine chambers, cramped, poorly-lit and airless, were less than salubrious. The two suites inserted in the upper space of the former Long Gallery are barely tall enough for an adult to stand upright in. Unheated and directly beneath the lead roof, they would have been very cold in winter, unbearably hot in summer.

In 1823 Wyatville was again commissioned to make further alterations to the house, which was clearly bursting at the seams and in desperate need of more service accommodation. He had no alternative but to extend, so he

Ill. 57.

designed a single-storey service wing to be added to the west side of the house at basement level. There exists a very elegant elevation drawing showing the

Ill. 58.
Ill. 59.

proposed extension, although not in the form it was finally built, and also a rather rough plan of the work, more or less as it was actually carried out. The extension contained more sleeping accommodation and a new servants' hall, which freed the old servants' hall (originally the Tudor Ale Cellar) to provide another dormitory. Wyatville perceived an enormous waste of space here, for the vaulted room was about 5.6m tall. By splitting it horizontally in two, he was able to make two dormitories. Moreover, he did away with the old cellar stairs, replacing them with a much smaller staircase, and used the upper part of the old stairs to sqeeze in yet another small room. The floor which had been inserted half way up the old Ale Cellar was now about level with the south wing of the basement, and this might have given him the idea of knocking through the old walls which divided the basement into two separate areas. In the Tudor house, as we have seen, to get any sort of private accommodation was something of an honour, so those high-ranking servants housed in the Yeomens' Lodgings were considered too grand to be associated with the functional side of the basement, which was kept quite separate. Although high-ranking servants were still housed in the old Yeomens' Lodgings (for example, the Steward lived in the south-east corner room), it was now considered more advantageous to have greater circulation in the basement than to worry about affronting the dignity of the servants.

Ill. 60.   Cutting through to the Yeomens' corridor on the south side of the house was relatively simple: in entailed smashing through two walls and curtailing the size of one of the Yeoman's Lodgings (labelled 4/13 on the phased plan). But cutting through to the Wine Cellar on the east side was far more complicated, for the cellar was almost a

Ill. 56. A mezzanine level suite above the Long Gallery. The staircase has been contrived in one of the window embrasures. Photo by Philip Dixon.

Ill. 57. The west elevation of the house, showing the service wing added c.1823. Photo by Chris Salisbury.

Ill. 58. Wyatville's elevation drawing of the west service extension.
By courtesy of Hon. Michael Willoughby and University of Nottingham Library (Mi P3/3/2)

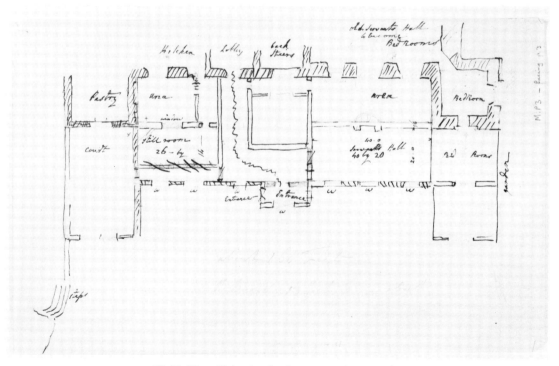

Ill. 59. Wyatville's plan for the west service extension
By courtesy of Hon. Michael Willoughby and University of Nottingham Library (Mi P3/3/1).

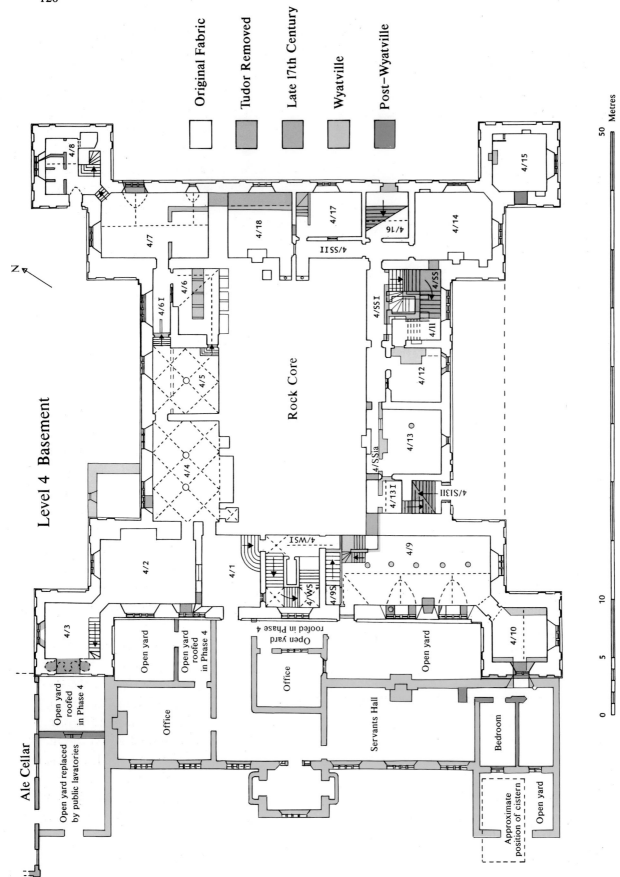

Level 4 Basement

Original Fabric

Tudor Removed

Late 17th Century

Wyatville

Post–Wyatville

Ale Cellar

Open yard replaced by public lavatories

Open yard roofed in Phase 4

Office

Open yard

Open yard roofed in Phase 4

4/3

4/2

4/1

4/4

4/5

4/6

4/6 I

4/7

4/8

4/18

4/17

4/15

4/14

4/16

4/SSII

4/SSI

4/SS

4/11

4/12

4/13

4/13 I

4/13III

4/SSIa

4/WSI

4/WS

4/9S

4/9SI

4/9

4/10

Rock Core

Office

Open yard roofed in Phase 4

Servants Hall

Open yard

Bedroom

Approximate position of cistern

Open yard

N

0   5   10   50
Metres

Ill. 60. Phased plan of the basement showing alterations made by Wyatville c.1823. Drawing by David Taylor.

metre lower. Wyatville's answer was to cut back one of the Yeomen's Lodgings (4/17) to make room for a short flight of stairs, then tunnel underground to reach the Wine Cellar (4/7). The upper part of the tunnel intruded into another of the Yeomen's lodgings (4/18), so he partitioned that off. Fortunately, the partition only reached as far as the window sill, so the room still had light. There might be an explanation for this dogged determination to connect the wine cellar with the basement south corridor. The old Saucery (4/6) and the narrow passage beside it were blocked off from the neighbouring Larder (4/5) and adapted for the storage of wine. Racks for the bottles were installed and the only window was blacked out. This created a cellar within a cellar, for the new storage space could only be reached from the main Wine Cellar next door (4/7). It must have been used to keep the most prized vintages, for a heavy iron door was fitted, making it, in effect, a strong-room for wine. However, it had blocked the only basement access to the main Wine Cellar: if the new entry had not been driven through, one could only have approached it from the floor above.

During the building campaign of the 1820s, Lord Middleton apparently toyed with the idea of remodelling the turret chambers. Among several design drawings initialled by Wyatville and dated 1823, is one which shows octagonal turrets crowned with coronets. On the reverse of the sheet is the same

Ill. 61.

Ill. 61. Wyatville's proposal for redesigning the turrets, dated 1823. Based on a drawing in the Middleton collection. (David Taylor) drawing with a plainer top and the written instruction 'omit the coronet'. The plan, fortunately, fell by the wayside. The only change to the turrets was the addition of chimney stacks to accommodate flues inserted into the towers. The stacks curve inwards to meet one another and share a cluster of chimney pots.

Ill. 62.

The 6th baron had other plans which did not materialize. He was clearly giving thought to outbuildings and cottages on the estate and a number of drawings and plans exist, some by different architects, which were never executed. Wyatville himself submitted proposals for a gate and lodges at Wollaton village. Two additions to the grounds were, however, made about this time. Lenton Lodge, a new gatehouse at one of the entries to the estate, was built following an Elizabethan gatehouse plan, probably drawn by Smythson himself. Wyatville is likely to have been responsible for the design of the Camellia House, situated south-west of the Hall, a building

Ill. 63.

Ill. 64.

Ill. 62. Curving chimney stacks were added to the turrets to serve new flues. Wyatville increased the number of fireplaces all over the house, particulary in the towers.

***Ill. 63.** Drawing of a gateway at Wollaton designed and drawn by J. and J.C. Buckler, May 1822. It was never built. By courtesy of Hon. Michael Willoughby and University of Nottingham Library (MiP 3/18/1)*

Ill. 64. The Camellia House was a great technical achievement when it was built c.1823. Lord Middleton is reputed to have spent the modern equivalent of £25,000 on plants. (Photo by Chris Salisbury)

which reflects the growing obsession of the age with the cultivation of exotic plants. The structure was in the vanguard of new technology, being prefabricated in iron and glass and predating the famous Crystal Palace by over a quarter of a century. It was made by Messrs. Jones and Clark of Birmingham, metallic hot house builders. They may have been responsible for the design of the heating system, which used collected rainwater to produce the necessary levels of humidity.

Worries over security

Ironically Wyatville, who inserted mezzanine chambers all over the house, seems to have removed an original mezzanine room on the ground floor. According to household inventories of 1599 and 1601, there was a mezzanine chamber over the inner chamber to the 'Garden' or 'Duke's' chamber, which was taken out to create the strong-room. He did, however insert another mezzanine level room here, below the floor. This came about in 1832 when, for a third time, the architect was brought in to alter the house. The previous year was marked by unrest over parliamentary reform. Reform riots had resulted in the burning of Nottingham castle in October 1831 and Wollaton Hall itself had been unsuccessfully attacked by the mob. Although these incidents effectively marked the end of the outbreak of unrest, Lord Middleton could hardly have foreseen this and, not surprisingly, was very worried about security. The new mezzanine level room was to be a secure muniment room to keep the baron's deeds and papers safe. It impinged on the upper space in the basement room of the north-east tower, but the ceiling here was fortunately very high. A brick vault was inserted into this space to form the floor of the new room, whose ceiling was also vaulted in brick. Stone shelves were put inside, so the room was effectively fireproof. It could only be reached by a trapdoor in the floor of the strongroom above, itself protected by a heavy iron door. Lord Middleton's valuables were about as safe as they could be.

Ill. 65.A secure muniment room was built between floors in 1832, when Lord Middleton was disturbed by the threat of civil unrest.

Nevertheless, the baron was still concerned. Bars were added to many of the lower storey windows and the possibility of a less passive defence of the house was considered. The 'armoury' installed before 1809 was perhaps more than merely a conceit, a nod towards the Romanticism which imbued much of the contemporary literature with Gothic Revivalism. For Lord Middleton kept a stout collection of weapons in his armoury and would not have been afraid to use them if necessary. To defend the Derby Road entrance to the park, Wyatville was asked to design 'two circular lodges something of the martello kind' with a secure ground floor, blind and inaccessible from outside. In a letter to the architect, Lord Middleton stipulated that 'they should flank each other, with narrow slip (sic.) windows to fire thro', similar to old Castles. Some sort of Battlements in unison with the ornaments of the house might be contrived, to hide a cannon on the top.' They were each to house a family in two-roomed tenements: the result was Beeston Lodge.

Lord Middleton's growing paranoia over civic unrest is reflected in further work carried out for reasons of security. The Tudor wainscotting in the Great Hall, despite being described as 'magnificent carved woodwork', was removed. It was seen as a liability in view of the recent 'deplorable example [the fire at Nottingham Castle] — how very soon a place may be consumed where there is dry wainscote.' Rather perversely, it was replaced and Wyatville submitted two alternative designs for Lord Middleton to choose from. At the same time Middleton asked that wainscotting in his study in the south-west corner chamber should also be removed and he requested some improvements to the Saloon, or sitting room. Instructions were given 'to take down all the wainscote in the Salloon, and to fit up that Room in character with the rest of this building'. In this case the wainscot was late 17th century, for the Dining

Ill. 66.

Ill. 66. A design drawing by Wyatville for wainscotting in the Great Hall, 1832. The drawing made two suggestions, one (to the left) on a flap which could be pulled down to reveal the right-hand design over the whole elevation. Lord Middleton indicated, in his own hand: 'We wish to decide upon this [ie. the right], having four divisions, Because we think it will light better, & be nearer the old panels in the former wainscot'.
By courtesy of Hon. Michael Willoughby and University of Nottingham Library (MiP3/15).

Ill. 67. The 'Saloon', or sitting room, after Wyatville's alterations of c.1832. Previously the Dining Parlour, it had both changed function and been extended: the window in this picture would originally have lit the 'Garden Stairs'. Photo by Philip Dixon

Parlour had been gutted in the fire of 1642. The baron also wished to increase the size of the room at the expense of 'the space of the steps going into the garden', (ie. the 'garden' stairs), adding 'if possible we may effect an exit to the Garden under the floor of the Salloon.' As a result of these requests, the Saloon took the shape it retains today, extending further west than its fore-runner. A central doorway in the north wall allowed direct access from the Great Hall and French windows were opened on to the terrace. The garden steps, taken out to extend the Saloon, were diverted from the terrace into the basement, so Lord Middleton also got his 'exit to the Garden under the floor of the Salloon'. The loss of the 'Garden Stairs' also removed the doorway to the study in the south-west corner chamber, so a new entry had to be contrived. This was achieved by a short corridor, created by partitioning off a section of the old Buttery. As with the new Dining Room, the Middletons were oblivious to their study being entered by a former service door: times had changed.

Ill. 67.

More Prospect Room Problems

The decorative pelmets added to the windows in the Propect Room, with their Regency-style *trompe l'oeil* drapery, suggest that the room had continued to enjoy rather elegant use. This conjecture might be confirmed by a letter of August 1830, in which Mr. C. Chouler, the acting steward, reported to Lord Middleton on the condition of the floor. It was clearly giving cause for alarm by sinking in the middle, and they were also curious to know how it related to the hammer beams in the Great Hall. Chouler had taken down the Great Hall ceiling to expose the joist arrangement above, no doubt in the process removing the plasterwork Sir Francis Willoughby had given the plasterer Ragge a bonus of £2 for in 1586. He refers to the dirty and dusty nature of the job, which may explain the plentiful supplies of beer which were apparently available to the 40-strong workforce, according to a letter left by one of their number, William Burton, who secreted it under the new floorboards for posterity. (It was discovered in 1954.) Chouler gave a reassuring report to his master, saying that although the construction of the floor was 'singular', the timber was in good condition. He had caused the workmen to 'force the parts [ie. the main joists] back into the wall', with limited success.

Ill. 33.

The main arches of the hammer beam roof had also been sinking, causing their joints to weaken. Iron braces were added to the apex of each arch to secure them to the joists above but, since these too were sinking, it was probably a wasted exercise. Finally the workmen replaced the Great Hall ceiling with timber panelling. Lord Middleton seems to have been less than convinced by Chouler's reassuring words, judging by underlining and comments in a different hand added to his letter. The steward commented that the hammer

Ill. 68.

Ill. 68. Details of hammer beam trusses in the Great Hall, showing a) pressure on the joints and b) one of the iron ties added in 1830 to the apex of the arches to hold up the Great Hall trusses.

beams in the Great Hall 'have very little connection with the floor above', adding that 'this is a fortunate circumstance, as it would not be wise to add to its [ie. the floor's] weight': this comment was underlined by the recipient. Chouler ended by saying he would know more in a few days' time, but added the assertion that there was no danger if 'every necessary caution is used against accident'. Clearly unconvinced, the other hand has appended a note at the bottom: 'it certainly would not be safe to have many people in the Prospect Room, such as dancing'.

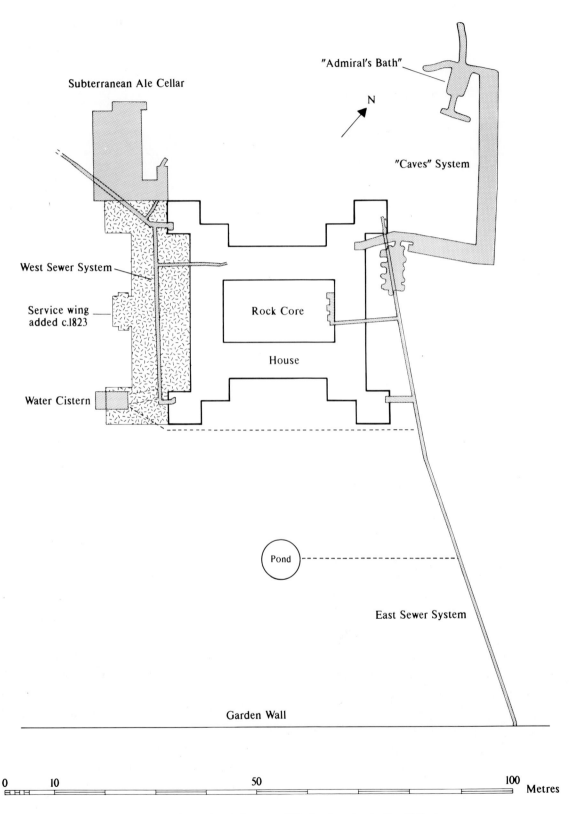

"Admiral's Bath"

N

"Caves" System

Subterranean Ale Cellar

West Sewer System

Service wing
added c.1823

Rock Core

House

Water Cistern

Pond

East Sewer System

Garden Wall

0   10   50   100   Metres

Ill. 69. Plan of the Underground Works. Drawing by David Taylor

Chapter 9: Wollaton's Subterranean Life

Ill. 69.

Ill. 70.

Ill. 71.

As they walk around the immediate vicinity of the house, most visitors are unaware that beneath their feet lie the vestiges of an essential aspect of the Tudor services: the drains. Wollaton has a remarkably well-preserved Elizabethan sewer system, which cleverly and invisibly removed waste from the house. Sanitation was provided by two separate underground drainage systems, one on the east and the other on the west side. From every garderobe (toilet) in the house, there was a sheer drop down vertical chutes within the thickness of the wall. At the bottom was a culvert which conveyed waste to one of the long main sewers. The entire system is constructed in brick, with barrel-vaulted roofs to the sewers and culverts. Distinct building breaks can be seen in the culvert walls, showing that the main passages were built independently of the house, perhaps as the building was nearing completion, then joined up to the rest of the system as the house was finished.

The sewer floors were designed to maintain a steady fall, with a slightly V-shaped dip in the brick floors so that liquid would easily have drained away. It might well have been common practice to flush out the culverts, where there is generally a steeper fall, by pouring water down the chutes, but in the main passages the slope is universally too gentle to ensure that this would remove solids. These must have been regularly and manually cleaned and are tall enough for a man to stand upright in. Both systems survive for considerable lengths but were cut short by later work, so it is impossible to say how they originally terminated: we may speculate that they ended in soakaways at a reasonable distance from the house. The eastern sewer was curtailed when the gardens were reformed during the 1680s, when it is likely that the system was no longer used for sewerage. Garderobes could become rather smelly, and were already going out of fashion when Wollaton was built: the 'close stool' concealing a chamber pot was becoming more commonly used and had become universal by Thomas and Cassandra's time. However, the western drain continued in use for drainage of the Ale Cellar to the north-west of the house, and later a kitchen sink.

The garderobes were removed from the house long ago, but the chutes are sited precisely where privies would be expected from Smythson's design plan (illustration 9). Each of the 'inner chambers' in the towers had a garderobe in the corner

Ill. 70. A culvert linking a chute in the S.E. tower with the main E. sewer.

and on the east side of the house there was an additional set of three garderobe chutes in the thickness of the central tower wall. These served a convenience on the leads, one off the Long Gallery on the first floor and one in each of the Painted Chambers on the ground floor. However, the use of private facilities was not confined to the family, for the staff had them too. In the basement of the south-east tower the Gardener's Chamber is likely to have had its own, and the Cook's Chamber in the north-west tower could technically have had one as well. Four of the five Yeomen's Lodgings shared two communal toilets off their corridor, but the fifth Lodging very likely had its own.

Ill. 71. The main passage in the E. sewer system. Photo by Chris Salisbury.

The drains were also connected to the cellars, where swilling and slopping out would have occurred regularly. The stone stairs which lead to the mezzanine Cook's Chamber stop short of the south-west corner, where the garderobe chute is located in the wall thickness. This might have been deliberately contrived to give access to a sink or slop-out in the corner of the pastry kitchen below, in an age when hygiene was so imperfectly appreciated.

On the west side the sewer system originally connected only with garderobe chutes in the towers, but two further culverts were added later. Probably during the time of Thomas and Cassandra Willoughby, a drain was connected to the newly-built Ale Cellar and, later still, another was inserted under the house to serve the kitchens (possibly a stone sink in the Larder). A brick-lined cistern just west of the south-west tower might date from the same period. It was designed to store water conveyed into it by drain-pipes from the roof. An overflow connects the top of the cistern with the south-west corner of the sewer so that, in the event of overfilling, surplus water would run into the drainage system. The western sewer had to be strengthened in parts, where later work was built over it. The south-west corner of the Ale Cellar overlies it, so the builders thought it wise to reinforce it here. One of the reinforcing ribs contained a sherd of pottery dating from the late 17th or early 18th century. A similar step was taken by Wyatville when his service extension was built above another part, although here only one point was strengthened.

Ill. 72.

The Subterranean Ale Cellar

One of the more important changes made by Thomas and Cassandra

West Elevation
Sewer And Underground Cellar System

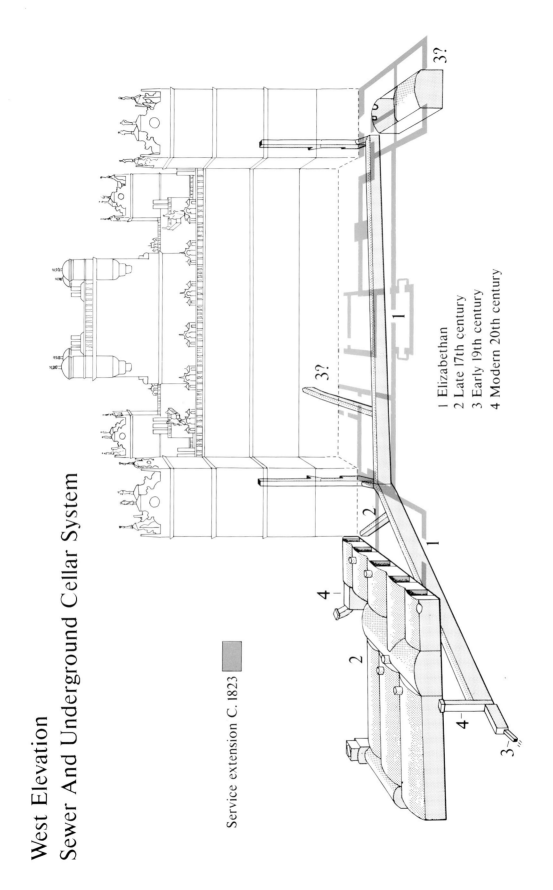

Service extension C. 1823

1 Elizabethan
2 Late 17th century
3 Early 19th century
4 Modern 20th century

Ill. 72. The west elevation of the house, showing the location of the Elizabethan sewer and the underground Ale Cellar, built c.1690. The blue lines indicate where the new servants' wing was added in c.1823. Drawing by David Taylor.

***Ill. 73.** Part of the subterranean ale cellar dating from Thomas and Cassandra's refurbishment of the house in the late 17th century. Photo by Chris Salisbury.*

Willoughby was to convert the Tudor Ale Cellar into a servants' hall. The loss was remedied by the construction of a much larger Ale Cellar by the north-west corner of the house (for its location, see illustrations 69 and 72). The building consists of a series of brick vaulted chambers and it runs northwards to a length of over 19 metres. The south front of the cellars formed a new facade facing the service courtyard, with a row of five doorways. Only this elevation and a very short section of the south-west corner could be seen above ground, for the rest was completely covered in earth. The intention was always that the cellars should be subterranean, for ventilation shafts were placed in the roof. The builders were no doubt anxious that the architectural impact of the house should not suffer from the close proximity of such a utilitarian structure. Most of the five wide doorways to the courtyard were blocked by Wyatville's service extension, which included a yard (marked 'court'), where one doorway was retained for access to the cellar. His design sketch for the extension shows the radiating steps which still exist by the south-west corner of the cellar. Wyatville's yard was built over when the house became a museum amd now houses public lavatories. At some time during the 20th century, one bay of the Ale Cellar was extended and two others altered to make a coal cellar.

Ill. 73.

Ill. 59.

The 'Caves' System

Ill. 74.

Ill. 75.

Ill. 76.

Ill. 77.

Ill. 78.

Ill. 79.

Beneath the ground on the east side of the house is a complex of wide passages and small chambers which has become popularly known as the 'caves' system or the 'Admiral's Bath' complex. The spaces have been tunnelled from the soft sandstone which forms the natural geology of the site, although most are lined in brick. In the absence of either documentary evidence or stylistic detail, it is impossible to date the complex, except to say that its entry certainly post-dates the original build of the house. Clues to its history and development, however, are suggested by its plan.

The complex is entered by a doorway cut through the wall of the Wine Cellar, where a flight of stone steps descends sharply. The original wall of the house was roughly hacked through and not made good. The steep descent was necessary to avoid the eastern sewer, whose floor crosses just inches above the staircase. As there is no sign of damage to the sewer, we must assume that the entry represents a very competent piece of surveying and engineering. At this point the stair passage is quite roughly cut from the sandstone, but when it reaches the bottom the passageways are lined with a brick barrel-vault. There is an irregular-shaped chamber cut from the natural rock off to the south-east, which has brick shelves for storing wine and is barred by an iron gate. As its doorway has been cut through the bricks of the passage wall, the room was added later. Recent and regular rock falls within this chamber demonstrate why it was necessary to face the greater part of the complex in brick.

Not far beyond, the passage widens and later turns northwards. Although both legs of the main L-shaped passage were furnished with brick thralls to store barrels, the use of this complex as an additional cellar for the storage of liquor was probably secondary to its main purpose, which was concerned with water supply. The main passage eventually links up with a system of narrower, more roughly cut passages approximately 30 metres away. The centrepiece of these is a large rock-cut cistern, popularly called the Admiral's Bath because of a tradition that one of the family, Rear Admiral Sir Nesbitt Willoughby (d.1849), bathed in it daily while resident at the Hall. The cistern fills naturally and is never dry: when the water table is particularly high, it overflows into another T-shaped cistern behind it. The presence of the Admiral's Bath might explain the motive for building the 'caves' complex.

Ill. 76. The staircase leading to the 'caves' system: the entry was cut through the wall of the Elizabethan Wine Cellar at a much later date.

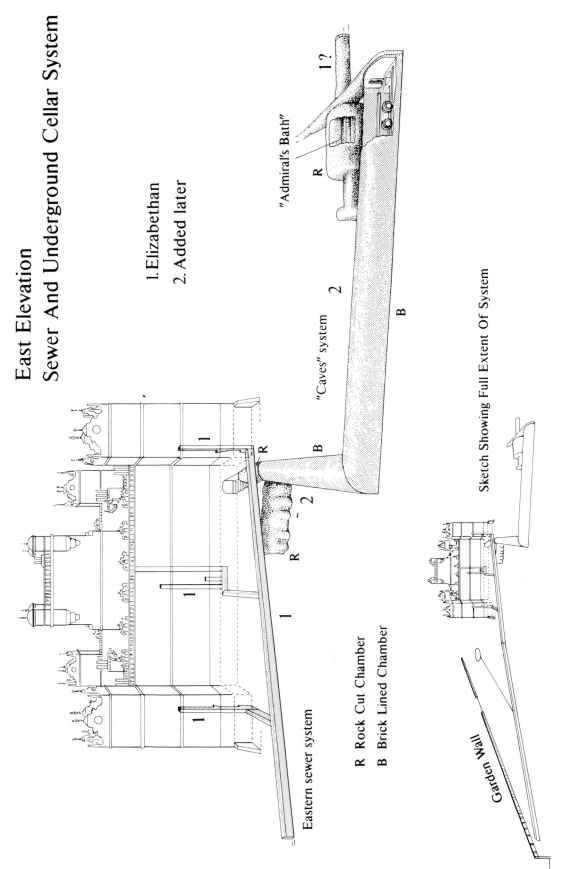

East Elevation
Sewer And Underground Cellar System

1. Elizabethan
2. Added later

"Admiral's Bath"

"Caves" system

R Rock Cut Chamber
B Brick Lined Chamber

Eastern sewer system

Sketch Showing Full Extent Of System

Garden Wall

Ill. 74. The east elevation of the house, showing the relationship of the eastern sewer and the 'caves' system to the building. Drawing by David Taylor.

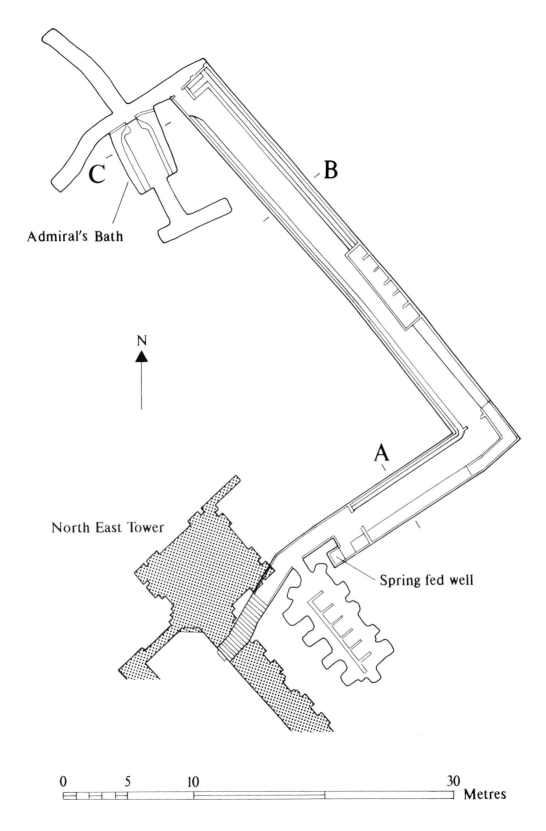

C

B

Admiral's Bath

N

A

North East Tower

Spring fed well

0   5   10   30
                                        Metres

Ill. 75. Plan of the 'caves' system.   Drawing by David Taylor

Ill. 77. View of the main passage in the 'caves' system, leading to the 'Admiral's Bath'. Photo by Chris Salisbury.

Ill. 78. The rock-cut cistern known as the 'Admiral's Bath'. Photo by Chris Salisbury.

Ill. 79. Rear-Admiral Sir Nesbitt Willoughby (d.1849). Family tradition claimed that he bathed daily in this cistern while staying at the hall. The fictional character Admiral Hornblower is reputed to have been based on him. By courtesy of Hon. Michael Willoughby.

The Admiral's Bath and its adjoining passages, two of which are blocked, are different in character from the rest of the complex. They do not follow a regular plan, as if the miners were following natural veins and fissures in the rock: it might be significant that the rock around the cistern itself seems quite stable, as if a particulary hard section had been chosen in which to fashion it. Its associated blocked passages, one running north and the other west, might represent earlier accesses to the cistern, or they might have led to others. Whilst it is impossible to date a rock-cut, featureless cavern, it could well be that the Admiral's Bath is part of a water storage system belonging to the original house, accessible only from outside by passages which became dangerous. Water supply to a house built on top of a hill must have been something of a problem, and it should be remembered that the Willoughby family fortune was partly based on successful coal-mining. Moreover, the creation of artificial caves has also been part of Nottingham's building tradition since the Middle Ages. The brick-lined passage leading to the 'Admiral's Bath' seems to make a bee-line to reach it, the L-shape being necessary to avoid its T-shaped overflow. The following interpretation of the 'caves' system therfore seems feasible. The Admiral's Bath area survives from an original water supply system, which might have been more extensive, but was inconvenient as it was only accessible from outside the house. A plan was therefore devised which would enable the water supply to be reached more directly from the house. The main passage of the complex also encompasses a natural spring-fed well, always full of clear water, whose inclusion might have been a happy accident. The new 'caves', with their cool, dark conditions, were also exploited as extra cellarage, which was later extended by the addition of a further chamber near the bottom of the stairs.

Epilogue: A new role for Wollaton

Despite their extensive programme of modernization, the Middleton family used Wollaton less and less during the latter part of the 19th century, preferring their Yorkshire residence at Birdsall. Few alterations were made to the house, although a bathroom was installed, rather oddly, in the well of the stairs which Thomas and Cassandra added to reach the leads more easily (see illustration 48).

In 1921 Sir Jesse Boot approached the 9th baron, making an offer for the estate, where he wished to site Nottingham University. He was refused, but in 1924 the 10th baron, pressed by death duties, agreed to sell the estate to Nottingham Corporation. At this time large country houses were becoming a liability; purchasers were hard to find and many mansions were falling into decay. Lord Middleton clearly wished, not only that the future of the buildings would be assured, but also that the people of Nottingham would benefit from access to the house and park. However, he died before the sale was concluded and it was left to the 11th baron to finish the business. The hall and park were sold for £200,000, while the park deer and armoury weapons were given to the city. In 1925 the Corporation recouped their investment by selling off some of the estate for new housing, keeping the rest for a public facility. The house was converted for use as a natural history museum, opened in 1926, and the 18th-century stables were subsequently converted to an industrial museum and art gallery. The City has maintained the fabric of the great building and the city stonemasons, who regularly repair and maintain Wollaton and other buildings belonging to the City Council, have their HQ in the Tudor Wine Cellar.

Permanent alterations made in connection with Wollaton's changed role have been surprisingly few. Although it is difficult for the visitor to imagine many of the rooms in their earlier contexts, beneath the museum displays the house remains essentially a Georgian interior inside a grand Elizabethan shell. On weekdays in term time it rings with the noise of children on school visits, many taking advantage of special educational facilities housed in Wyatville's servants' extension. At weekends Wollaton Park, its lake and buildings, attract families and is often the venue for special events. Wollaton is presently under review, but whatever decisions are made concerning its future, its role as an asset for the people of Nottingham will remain paramount and it will doubtless continue to hold a special place in their affections.

Ill. 80. One of Wollaton's more recent occupants.

Select Bibliography

Primary Sources

Middleton Collection, Manuscripts and Special Collections Dept., Local History Section, Hallward Library, University of Nottingham.

R.I.B.A. *Catalogue of the drawings, Collection of the R.I.B.A.* vol. 8 ed. M. Richardson.

Wollaton Hall (the building).

Secondary Sources

Abbreviations:
TTSN: *Transactions of the Thoroton Society of Nottinhgamshire*
HMC: Historical Manuscripts Commission

Airs M., *The Tudor and Jacobean Country House: A Building History* (Alan Sutton, Stroud, 1995)

Britton J., *Architectural Antiquities of Great Britain,* vol. II (London, 1809).

Builder The, (13th April, 1889).

Camden W., *Britannia*, (London, 1695).

Cameron A., *Sir Henry Willoughby of Wollaton*, TTSN vol. 74, 1970, pp.10-80.

Chandos, Cassandra Duchess of , *History of the Willoughby Family.*

   Vol. 1. *Middleton Manuscripts*, ed HMC (London, 1911).

   Vol. II. *The Continuation of the History of the Willoughby Family,* ed. A.C.Wood, University of Nottingham Shakespeare Head Press, (Nottingham, 1958).

Durant D., *Wollaton Hall, a Rejected Plan*, TTSN, vol. 76, 1972, pp. 13-16.

Girouard M., *Robert Smythson and the Elizabethan Country House,* Yale University Press (New Haven and London, 1983).

Girouard M., *Hardwick Hall*, (National Trust, 1989)

Hodson J.M., *The Wollaton Estate and the Civil War 1643-47*, TTSN vol. 65, 1961, pp. 3-15.

Linstrum D., *Sir Jeffrey Wyatville, Architect to the King,* Oxford University Press (Oxford, 1972).

Marshall P., *Wollaton Hall: An Archaeological Survey* (Nottingham Civic Society, Nottingham 1996)

Rossel P.E., *The Building of Wollaton Hall, 1580-88*, Unpublished MA thesis, 2 vols., University of Sheffield (1957).

Serlio S., *Architecture*, Lib. I (1566).

Smith R. S., *Sir Francis Willoughby of Wollaton Hall*, (City of Nottingham, 1988).

Strauss S.M., *A Short History of Wollaton and Wollaton Hall,* (City of Nottingham, 1978).

Stevenson, W.H. (ed.), *Middleton Manuscripts*, (HMC Report, London, 1911).

Thoroton R. *The Antiquities of Nottinghamshire*, (London, 1677).